MAINSTREAMING
FEMINIST RESEARCH FOR
TEACHING RELIGIOUS STUDIES

MAINSTREAMING
FEMINIST RESEARCH FOR
TEACHING RELIGIOUS STUDIES

EDITED BY

ARLENE SWIDLER & WALTER E. CONN

COLLEGE THEOLOGY SOCIETY

RESOURCES IN RELIGION • 2

UNIVERSITY
PRESS OF
AMERICA

LANHAM • NEW YORK • LONDON

To our favorite mainstreamers

Leonard Swidler
and
Joann Wolski Conn

CONTENTS

SERIES EDITORS' PREFACE   vii

PREFACE   ix

1. HOW TO MAINSTREAM FEMINIST STUDIES BY RAISING QUESTIONS:
   THE CASE OF THE INTRODUCTORY COURSE   1
   June O'Connor

2. FEMINISM AND WORLD RELIGIONS   11
   Denise Lardner Carmody

3. TO SET THE RECORD STRAIGHT: BIBLICAL WOMEN'S STUDIES   21
   Elisabeth Schüssler Fiorenza

4. RECOVERING WOMEN'S HISTORY: EARLY CHRISTIANITY   33
   Rosemary Rader

5. WOMEN IN AMERICAN CATHOLIC HISTORY   45
   Arlene Swidler

6. FEMINIST THOUGHT AND SYSTEMATIC THEOLOGY   53
   Pauline Turner and Bernard Cooke

7. FEMINIST ETHICS IN THE CHRISTIAN ETHICS CURRICULUM   65
   Margaret A. Farley

8. THE FEMINIST TURN IN SOCIAL ETHICS   77
   Daniel C. Maguire

SERIES EDITORS' PREFACE

The College Theology Society co-publishes **CTS RESOURCES IN RELIGION** with University Press of America as part of its commitment to scholarship and effective teaching. This series makes available important resources which reflect the traditional interests and focus of the Society including Catholic theology and life, the broader Christian tradition, and universal religious experience as well as creative teaching in college and university settings.

The Research and Publications Committee of the CTS has sole editorial responsibility for the selection, design, and production of **CTS RESOURCES IN RELIGION, CTS STUDIES IN RELIGION**, and **CTS REPRINTS IN RELIGION**. Further information regarding these series can be found in the October 1983 number of the *CSR Bulletin* and any changes will be announced there in future issues. The sale and distribution of the volumes in these three series are the responsibility of University Press of America.

The editors are grateful to the members of the Research and Publications Committee, to the officers and board of the CTS, and to the others who contributed to the editorial and production process. We also express our thanks for the personal support given by our colleagues at Marquette University and Saint Joseph's University. Special acknowledgement is made of the services rendered by Susan Wilkes of Saint Joseph's University Press and by Terri Boddorff of UPA.

Managing Editor
Joseph F. Gower
Saint Joseph's University
Philadelphia, PA   19131

Chair, Publications Committee
Robert Masson
Marquette University
Milwaukee, WI   53233

PREFACE

A mere fifteen or twenty years ago anyone interested in the image and role of women in religion could easily have kept up on all the significant new research coming out in that entire area. Since then the scholarly output on women and religion has so increased and so deepened that it is difficult to stay on top of current developments in even a rather narrow specialization. Some teachers have prepared and taught courses on women and religion, but for the vast majority of people in religious studies, who maintain a sympathetic interest in the new feminist scholarship but whose main energies are focused elsewhere, keeping abreast has become absolutely impossible.

As feminist scholarship has blossomed, its significance has also heightened. In the beginning it was generally assumed that women's studies offered intriguing details and illuminating examples worth integrating into other courses—what some feminists have referred to with a touch of cynicism as the "add women and stir" approach. Then, as feminist theorizing developed, the recognition grew that omission of women's experiences and insights in any college religion course resulted in a presentation which was unbalanced, incomplete, distorted. Most recently feminist scholars have actually challenged many of the basic suppositions of the various religious and theological disciplines and insisted that the methods themselves must be corrected. Although the need for sharply focused scholarship and special courses on women and religion remains and even grows, teachers are now aware that some of this research and insight must be directed into mainstream courses.

The College Theology Society, along with its journal *Horizons* (published at Villanova University), has thus found itself with two tasks. First, it has long encouraged specialized feminist scholarship; its annual meetings have included sessions on women and religion, and *Horizons* has published not only feminist research but also syllabi for courses on women and religion and the results of a survey of teachers of such courses. At the same time, through *Horizons* the Society has also been attempting to complement this work by publishing a series of articles designed to enable non-specialists to integrate the findings of feminist scholarship into their own mainstream courses. It is this series which is now presented here in a single volume.

The project was begun by consulting with college teachers from a variety of institutions across the country to see which undergraduate courses would most benefit by essays such as these. The suggestions sent in were for the most part rather easily divided into the eight categories found here: introduction to religion, world religions, Bible, early Christianity, American (i.e., U.S.) Catholic history, systematic theology, personal ethics, and social ethics.

Authors for these eight essays were chosen with much care. Not only did we need people who were established scholars in the fields they were presenting, but they had to be committed to and knowledgeable in women's studies as well. And—an equally important criterion—our writers had to have had experience teaching the relevant courses on an undergraduate level. This is not to say, of course, that much of what is said here will not be extremely useful for the graduate or seminary professor, or that high school teachers will not find guidance here as well, but our main focus is on undergraduate teaching.

The essays are designed to help undergraduate teachers feel at home in the feminist scholarship of their areas—to get some sense of who the important writers are and what they are saying, to follow current trends in feminist scholarship. Whenever possible our writers have tried to present concrete help: class projects that they have themselves found effective, ideas for research papers and book reports, evaluations of current texts, and suggestions of articles and books for assigned reading. All of our writers have found that the inclusion of feminist materials and approaches in their own mainstream courses has sparked excitement; these essays are their attempt to share their experiences with other teachers.

Many people have helped with this project. We would like to thank the respondents to our initial questionnaire, our authors, and, especially, Teresa Byrne for her editorial assistance.

Arlene Swidler
Walter E. Conn
Villanova University
Villanova, PA   19085

1

HOW TO MAINSTREAM FEMINIST STUDIES BY RAISING QUESTIONS: THE CASE OF THE INTRODUCTORY COURSE

June O'Connor

"Religious Myths and Rituals," a course I teach once a year, is a lower division undergraduate course designed to introduce students to the academic study of religion. Its purpose is to acquaint students with the wide range of scholarly views regarding the meanings, origins, and functions of religion, the mythic and ritual components of religion, the widespread presence of religious symbols, the metaphoric character of religious language, diverse crosscultural images of transcendence, sacrality, and the like. In order to introduce the theoretical materials or to test or illuminate them, we focus on the specific religious expressions of American Indian and African tribal societies.[1] Although examples from other religions are cited in the course of class lectures, these two tribal cultural settings serve as our primary reference points for understanding the phenomenon of religion.

On the course syllabus and early in the quarter, I articulate the following questions as a way of describing the task of the course: What is religion? What are the origins and functions of religion? What can we learn about myths and mythologies and the functions they have in human experience? Why do rituals arise in human behavior? (How do they take shape and what are they for?) Do any of the myths and rituals of traditional, tribal religions have any bearing on contemporary American life? How might we discern the meaning of religious symbols? What are some of the predominant myths and rituals that both reflect and affect our own lives as individuals or as a people (as Christians, Jews, Buddhists, atheists—as students, Americans, Westerners, as women or men)?

In addition to these questions, I invite the students to add to the list questions of their own and I encourage their question-asking inclina-

[1] This is one of three introductory courses in the Program in Religious Studies at the University of California, Riverside. The other two are Introduction to Eastern Religions and Introduction to Western Religions. Thus I make no effort to cover Hinduism, Buddhism, Judaism, Christianity, or Islam in my introductory course on the phenomenology of religion.

June O'Connor is Associate Professor of Religious Studies at the University of California, Riverside (Riverside, CA 92521). She is the author of The Quest for Political and Spiritual Liberation: A Study in the Thought of Sri Aurobindo Ghose (Rutherford, NJ: Fairleigh Dickinson University Press, 1977), and of articles in The Journal of Religious Ethics, Horizons, Listening: Journal of Religion and Culture, and The Christian Century. She is currently President of the American Academy of Religion, Western Region.

tions at various points in the quarter—during lectures and discussions, of course, and also in quizzes and exams. (For example, in a quiz on the book *Black Elk Speaks*, one question they face is: What questions does the book provoke in your own mind? Does it make you wonder? If so, about what? If Black Elk were to visit our class, what might you ask him?) I urge them in this endeavor to listen to everyone and everything: the authors, lectures, films, one another, nature, themselves—and to let the wonderings and the ponderings surface from their encounter with these sources. I urge them to approach the course as a time to see and to hear new things and to see and to hear old things in new ways.

I draw upon sociological, anthropological, and psychological theories as well as philosophical, phenomenological, historical and theological points of view. Thus, in a consideration of the meaning of religion, for example, students are exposed to definitions that come from Freud, Jung, Tillich, Marx, Durkheim, Otto, Eliade, (Ninian) Smart, and others. They are in this way exposed to views of religion that are antagonistic and sympathetic, eastern and western, humanistic and transcendental, doctrinal and ethical, critically reflective and experientially descriptive.

I place a high value on questions, believing with Suzanne Langer[2] that the contributions of a generation are to be discovered more by the questions raised than by the answers given or the achievements offered. For questions reveal our assumptions and our concerns, our views and our values. Thus, early in the class I not only identify the agenda of the course by formulating questions, I also engage students in naming the questions they bring with them.

In this context of question-asking, it is possible to highlight questions about women in religious contexts and women's religious experience in the religious traditions. For example: What is it like to be a woman in a tribal culture? What images of women are conveyed in the religious myths of a tribe under consideration? What do these myths tell us about who women are, where women come from, and what women are called to become? What do rituals communicate regarding women's status, needs, abilities? Are women and "the feminine" portrayed in images of the sacred and the divine or are such images reserved only for male divinities? What expectations are placed on women religiously and socially? What attitudes are proclaimed about women, about their power and authority, about sexuality, celibacy, marriage, maternity, and divorce? What opportunities are women able to pursue, independently of what is expected of them? How do individual tribal women describe themselves, their experience, their lives? What are their struggles, their sufferings, their disappointments? What are their hopes, their dreams, their aspirations?

[2] *Philosophy in a New Key: A Study in the Symbolism of Reason, Rite, and Art* (Cambridge: Harvard University Press, 1942).

It is important also to raise methodological questions. One way to do this is to suggest that by using the terms "man" and "male" generically, we are really overindulging in synecdoche.[3] "The male" has been made equivalent to "the human" so often that many of us have mistaken the part for the whole. We have assumed that the part represented the whole and thus rendered meaning accurately; when in fact what is portrayed is partial and incomplete, and thus, inaccurate. Feminist studies of thought, culture, and society press us to notice our exclusive perspectives and preferences, our noninclusive practices and policies. Men are commonly seen as the norm for understanding a culture. Women are then studied as parts of the culture, accommodated into the study rather than studied as active agents and participants. One of the features of our time, one of the contributions of our generation, is the asking of a cluster of questions that give new attention to women. Historians, theologians, social scientists, and literary scholars are asking in abundance questions that highlight the presence and the experience of women in every culture, in every context. They are also asking questions about *the ways we approach our materials*, seeking to highlight and to eliminate the bias on behalf of men that informs so much of our thought and research.

Questions about women are not the sole focus of the course I describe which is on the phenomenology of religion, not women and religion. Yet the questions about women's experiences and about our androcentric methods of inquiry are offered here as an illustration of ways in which scholarship on women and feminist thinking about religion can be integrated or mainstreamed into an established introductory course.

Core Bibliography

Instructors who wish to acquaint themselves with scholarship on women and religion will gain familiarity with a range of issues and methods of approach through study of the following sources. Because anthropologists are indispensable sources of information for understanding religious data in tribal cultures, anthropological materials as well as those of scholars in religion are cited heavily in this essay.

Sherry Ortner's essay, "Is Female to Male as Nature is to Culture?" in Michele Rosaldo and Louise Lamphere, eds., *Woman, Culture, and Society* (Stanford University Press, 1974), pp. 67-87, is an excellent starting point for two reasons. First, Ortner offers an intriguing and meritorious theory that uncovers "the underlying logic of cultural thinking that assumes the inferiority of women." Thus Ortner addresses and

---

[3] Synecdoche is a figure of speech by which a part is put for the whole (the sail for the ship, man for all human beings), or the whole for a part (the year for the fall, man for a particular class and race of men).

analyzes the heart of the matter. Second, she presents a clear view of the task of the scholarly study of women by differentiating three tasks requiring attention. There is the task of *direct observation* of women's activities, contributions, power, influence. There is also the task of *cultural analysis* wherein specific ideologies, symbolizations, and social-structural arrangements pertaining to women are considered. Finally, there is the task of inquiring and theorizing about the *universality* of culturally attributed second-class status of women in every society. In her essay Ortner addresses the universality question, though she acknowledges the importance and affirms the value of the other two tasks as well.

Edwin Ardener's "Belief and the Problem of Women" in Jean S. La Fontaine, ed., *The Interpretation of Ritual: Essays in Honour of A. I. Richards* (London: Tavistock, 1972), pp. 135-58, raises the methodological question inviting us to both reflect on our assumptions and to revamp our approaches of study.

Readings specifically oriented to scholarship in religion with a concern for the religious lives of women are increasing regularly. Several articles address the origins of this field (often named "women and religion"), methodologies recommended and employed, and agendas to be addressed. See Gayle Graham Yates, "Spirituality and the American Feminist Experience," *Signs: Journal of Women in Culture and Society* 9/1 (1983), 59-72; Rita Gross and Nancy Auer Falk's "Introduction: Patterns in Women's Religious Lives" in a book edited by them, *Unspoken Worlds: Women's Religious Lives in Non-Western Cultures* (San Francisco: Harper & Row, 1980), pp. xi-xviii; Carol Christ and Judith Plaskow, "Introduction: Womanspirit Rising" in a book edited by them, *Womanspirit Rising: A Feminist Reader in Religion* (San Francisco: Harper and Row, 1979), pp. 1-17; Rita Gross, "Androcentrism and Androgyny in the Methodology of History of Religions" in a book she edited, *Beyond Androcentrism: New Essays on Women and Religion* (Missoula, MT: Scholars Press, 1977), pp. 7-21; Rita Gross, "Methodological Remarks on the Study of Women in Religion: Review, Criticism, and Redefinition" in Judith Plaskow and Joan Arnold, eds., *Women in Religion* (rev. ed.; Missoula, MT: Scholars Press, 1974), pp. 153-65. Essays more theological in origin are Valerie Saiving's 1960 landmark essay, "The Human Situation: A Feminine View," reprinted in *Womanspirit Rising*, pp. 25-42; and Judith Plaskow's "The Feminist Transformation of Theology" in *Beyond Androcentrism*, pp. 23-33.

Given the title of my course, "Religious Myths and Rituals," we spend a good portion of our time examining examples of myths and rituals and theories about their meanings, purposes, and functions. Because Mircea Eliade's *Sacred and Profane* has been a constant in the course for introducing students to these topics, I was fascinated to discover Kathryn Allen Rabuzzi's *The Sacred and the Feminine* (New York: Seabury, 1982). There Rabuzzi explores the Myth of Happily Ever After which has been a dominant myth received by modern western women—and perhaps by women of other times and cultures as well. Rabuzzi utilizes Eliadian themes of sacred space, symbol, cosmization and ritual enactment as ways of illuminating the experience and mythological world views imposed upon or embraced by numerous women.

One of my goals in the course is to insure that students learn about the theories and behaviors that come to us from scholars, field observers, and the personal testimony of religious practitioners. Another goal is to have students think about the mythic and ritual dimensions of their own lives. To this end, they are given the following assignment toward the end of the quarter.

DIRECTIONS: Choose A or B. A. Mark Schorer writes: "Myths are the instruments by which we continually struggle to make our experience intelligible to ourselves. A myth is a large, controlling image that gives philosophical meaning to the facts of ordinary life."[4] Using this statement as a working definition of myth, write an essay in which you incorporate discussion of the following: 1. Describe one myth that you see to be operative in your life as an individual or in our lives together as a group. 2. Is the myth a "religious myth" or a "secular myth"? Explain. 3. How does this myth function (what does it do to people, for people)? 4. Do you notice any ritual or ceremonial expressions to this myth? 5. In what way(s) does the myth serve to enlarge one's understanding of life? 6. In what way(s) does the myth—or might it—confine and limit that understanding?

B. We have examined ritual as a form of communication and mode of expression that engages the whole person, physically, intellectually, emotionally, imaginatively, spiritually. Using this point of view as a working description of ritual, write an essay in which you incorporate discussion of the following: 1. Describe one ritual that is a part of your life. 2. Is this a "religious ritual" or a "secular ritual"? Explain. 3. How does this ritual function (what does it do to people, for people)? 4. To what myth does this ritual refer, in what mythic context is the ritual meaningful? 5. In what way(s) does the ritual benefit the participants? 6. In what way(s) does the ritual—or might it—constrict and limit its participants?

Students are instructed to incorporate class materials into their essays as appropriate (such as readings, films, lectures, handouts) for purposes of defining their terms, using comparisons or contrasts to make their points, and the like.

[4]"The Necessity of Myth" in Henry A. Murray, ed., *Myth and Mythmaking* (New York: George Braziller, 1960), p. 355.

This assignment is one of the most satisfying aspects of the course, for both the students and for me. For them, because it brings home in an experiential way just what the course is about; and for me, because I discover in a fresh and convincing way just how much they have come to understand the mythic and ritual aspects of human existence. The exercise thus requires them to *think with* the tools of the class and not to rest satisfied with learning what those tools (theories, definitions, descriptions) are. It is not enough to master what others have said. They must think on their own.

Theologian Penelope Washbourn has addressed the place of ritual in women's experience in a manner both illuminating and provocative. "Becoming Woman: Menstruation as Spiritual Challenge" in *Womanspirit Rising*, pp. 246-58, is an analysis rich with insight. Washbourn's book, *The Seasons of Woman: Song, Poetry, Ritual, Prayer, Myth, Story* (San Francisco: Harper & Row, 1979) is a compilation of many different types of literature through which women express their own spiritual sensibilities about their identities as women. *Becoming Woman: The Quest for Wholeness in Female Experience* is Washbourn's autobiographical work in which she identifies ten crisis points in the life of a woman and examines their religious significance. Together Rabuzzi and Washbourn extend mythic and ritual mirrors through which contemporary women can get a new angle of vision on their lives.

Collections of myths about woman as creator, as nature, as ancestral mother, as teacher of culture are available in Merlin Stone's *Ancient Mirrors of Womanhood: Our Goddess and Heroine Heritage* (2 vols.; New York: New Sibylline Books, 1979). Given the design of my course, I am particularly interested in her sections on African and American Indian sources. The scope of these volumes is broad, incorporating (Asian) Indian, Sumerian, Egyptian, Japanese, Chinese, Scandinavian, Mexican, and Greek materials. Mircea Eliade's *From Primitives to Zen* (New York: Harper and Row, 1967) and Barbara Sproul's *Primal Myths* (San Francisco: Harper and Row, 1979) also offer wide-ranging collections of myths that can inform us of views and values regarding women.

For bibliographies on studies about American Indian and African views by and about women, see a review essay by Rayna Green, "Native American Women," *Signs: Journal of Women in Culture and Society* 6/2 (1980), 248-67. Green opens her essay by acknowledging the great preponderance of anthropological literature on Native American women; studies psychological and sociological in nature are next in volume, with historical materials following fourth. If Green were to categorize these materials according to work done by scholars of religion, the list would, I trust, be short indeed. For insight into the religious perceptions, understandings, experiences, myths, and rituals of Native American and African peoples, we remain to a great extent dependent on social-scientific studies. Hopefully the absence of materials on the religious dimension of women's experience will be mitigated by further work from historians of religion and not only from anthropologists, sociologists and psychologists. A new publication, *Journal of Feminist Studies in Religion* (first issue expected Fall 1984), will begin to fill this yawning need. Margaret Strobel's review essay, "African Women," *Signs: Journal of Women in Culture and Society* 8/1 (1982), 109-31, assists religious studies scholars by singling out materials on "religion, ritual, and ideology" (127-30). Laura Kratochvil and Shauna Shaw have compiled *African Women—A Select Bibliography* (Cambridge: African Studies Centre, 1974) which contains a section devoted to "Religion and Ritual."

Relevant Articles

Martha Binford's "Julia: An East African Diviner" (*Unspoken Worlds*, pp. 3-21) is a wonderful narrative of surprise, suspense, and discovery heightened by Binford's interpretative and anecdotal skills. Here we meet a unique, individual woman who is portrayed in all of her particularity and concreteness.

Articles that study cultural systems and social patterns as they pertain to African women are the following: Anita Spring, "Epidemiology of Spirit Possession Among the Luvale of Zambia" in Judith Hoch-Smith and Anita Spring, eds., *Women in Ritual and Symbolic Roles* (New York: Plenum, 1978), pp. 165-90; J. S. La Fontaine, "Ritualization of Women's Life Crises in Bugisu" in J. S. La Fontaine, ed., *The Interpretation of Ritual*, pp. 159-86; Judith Hoch-Smith, "Radical Yoruba Female Sexuality" in *Women in Ritual and Symbolic Roles*, pp. 245-67; Susan Reynolds Whyte, "Men, Women and Misfortune in Bunyole" in Pat Holden, ed., *Women's Religious Experience* (Totowa, NJ: Barnes and Noble, 1983), pp. 175-92; Elizabeth Tonkin, "Women Excluded? Masking and Masquerading in West Africa" in *Women's Religious Experience*, pp. 163-74; Marion Kilson, "Women in Traditional African Religions," *Journal of Religion in Africa* 8/2 (1976), 133-43.

Mary Daly offers an ethical analysis and critique of some African puberty rites in "African Genital Mutilation: The Unspeakable Atrocities" in her *Gyn/Ecology: The Metaethics of Radical Feminism* (Boston: Beacon, 1978), pp. 153-77.

Two informative pieces on African female deities include Joseph Murphy's "Oshun the Dancer" in Carl Olson, ed., *The Book of the Goddess Past and Present: An Introduction to Her Religion* (New York: Crossroad, 1983), pp. 190-201, and Hans E. Hauge, "Loa, The Sun-Deity of the Iraqi People," E. Allardt, ed., *Temenos* 7 (1971), 50-57.

Ake Hultkranz has a clear and teachable essay on "The Religion of the Goddess in North America" in *The Book of the Goddess Past and*

Present, pp. 202-16. Marla Powers writes on "Menstruation and Reproduction: An Oglala Case" in *Signs: Journal of Women in Culture and Society* 6/1 (1980), 54-65. See also Mary Ann Sheridan and Daniel Sheridan, "Changing Woman and the Dis-ease of the Navajo: Psychological and Historical Perspective," *Anima* 6/2 (Spring 1980), 84-95.

Judith Todd sees similarities in Native American and contemporary feminist spirituality. See "On Common Ground: Native American and Feminist Spirituality Approaches in the Struggle to Save Mother Earth" in *The Politics of Women's Spirituality: Essays on the Rise of Spiritual Power Within the Feminist Movement* (Garden City, NY: Anchor/Doubleday, 1981), pp. 430-45. (An excellent film on Native American attitudes toward the land, "Sacred Ground," is available from New Visions, P. O. Box 599, Aspen, CO 81611.) Annemarie Shimony writes of "Women of Influence and Prestige Among the Native American Iroquois" in *Unspoken Worlds*, pp. 243-59.

Parabola, a journal that focuses on myth and tradition, has published many lovely stories about individual native American experiences. Don Talayesva narrates a childbirth ritual from the point of view of the child (an old man born in 1890) who has heard and remembered the stories about his birth. See "Twins Twisted Into One," *Parabola* 4/3 (1979), 6-12. Sister Maria Jose Hobday, whose mother was of Seneca Iroquois descent, describes her Native American roots in "Strung Memories," *Parabola* 4/4 (1979), 4-11. An interview with Judy Swamp in "A Woman's Ways," *Parabola* 5/4 (1980), 52-61, elicits the views of a contemporary Mohawk woman. Terry Tafoya depicts a Pacific Northwest ceremony in "Dancing with Dash-Kayah: The Mask of the Cannibal Woman," *Parabola* 6/3 (1981), 6-11.

Books for Reviews and Reports

Denise Paulme, ed., *Women of Tropical Africa*, trans. H. M. Wright (Berkeley: University of California Press, 1963); Audrey I. Richards, *Chisungu: A Girl's Initiation Ceremony Among the Bemba of Northern Rhodesia* (London: Faber and Faber, 1956). A companion volume with initial comment by A. I. Richards is Hans Cory's *African Figurines: Their Ceremonial Use in Puberty Rites in Tanganyika* (London: Faber and Faber, 1956). Henry John Drewel and Margaret Thompson Drewel have graced us with a study of Yoruba myth and ritual accompanied by a glorious array of photographs in *Gelede: Art and Female Power Among the Yoruba* (Bloomington: Indiana University Press, 1983).

Carolyn Niethammer has been acclaimed for her *Daughters of the Earth: The Lives and Legends of American Indian Women* (New York: Macmillan, 1977). Chapter 10 of Niethammer's book explicitly addresses "Religion and Spirituality."

Autobiographies are wonderful for access to unfamiliar cultures. See Gladys A. Reichard, *Dezba: Woman of the Desert* (Glorieta, NM: Rio Grande Press, 1971); Alvaro Estrada, *Maria Sabina: Her Life and Chants*, trans. and notated by Henry Munn (Santa Barbara, CA: Ross-Erikson, 1981); Polingaysi Qoyawayma, *No Turning Back* (Albuquerque: University of New Mexico Press, 1964); Helen Sekaquaptewa, *Me and Mine* (Tucson: University of Arizona Press, 1969); and Ruth Underhill, *Autobiography of a Papago Woman* (Maria Chona), (Menasha, WI: The American Anthropological Association, 1936); Nancy Lurie, *Mountain Lone Woman* (Ann Arbor: University of Michigan Press, 1961).[5]

In *Peyote Hunt: The Religious Pilgrimage of the Huichol Indians* (Ithaca, NY: Cornell University Press, 1974), Barbara G. Myerhoff briefly discusses the goddess in the Huichol pantheon and the participation of women in Huichol life and art. The *Art of the Huichol Indians* edited by Kathleen Berrin (New York: Fine Arts Museums of San Francisco/Harry N. Abrams, 1978) is a lovely companion volume filled with colored photographs. Peter Furst's film "To Find Our Life: The Peyote Hunt of the Huichols of Mexico" (University of California Extension Media Center, Berkeley, CA 94720), provides a wonderful illustration of the mythic and ritual dimensions of Huichol religion, though the feminine presence, whether human or divine, is not prominent.

Evaluation of Current Texts

In the past ten years that I have taught "Religious Myths and Rituals," required texts have varied. I normally require four or five common readings and in addition require a book report on an outside reading (from a bibliography I distribute in class). Mircea Eliade's *Sacred and Profane* is a proven winner and though I have shelved it from time to time out of my need for a change and student discontent with its repetitive character, I have recalled it from the shelf and required it again and again. For Eliade evokes thought and provokes discussion on issues central to the course. (Besides, I inform my students, repetition is a mark of effective teaching.) *Black Elk Speaks* is a favorite, a course constant and a lovely, illuminating, insightful, impressive, and charming book. Eliade the scholar and Black Elk the holy man render us wonderful companion pieces on the character of religious experience, the presence and purpose of symbol, the meaning of myth, the role of ritual.

Neither of them incorporate feminist questions nor women's experience as priority concerns. But such issues can be integrated by the class instructor who is willing to do two things: (1) some homework

[5] See also Gretchen M. Bataille and Kathleen Mullen Sands' study of autobiography, *American Indian Women: Telling Their Lives* (Lincoln: University of Nebraska Press, 1984). Essays which comprise the book are supplemented by an extensive (51 page) annotated bibliography.

studying the literature on women and religion and on feminist questions in religion (I hope this article facilitates that process); and (2) raise questions such as those identified in this article, questions about the experience of women in specific religious cultures and questions about our methods of inquiry and their commonly androcentric framework.

Books focusing on Native American religions are increasing in number. Materials I have tapped as required undergraduate texts (and all can be read with a feminist eye) have included the following: Ruth B. Underhill, *Red Man's Religion: Beliefs and Practices of the Indians North of Mexico* (Chicago: University of Chicago Press, 1965); Sam D. Gill, *Native American Religions: An Introduction* (Belmont, CA: Wadsworth, 1982); Barbara Tedlock and Dennis Tedlock, eds., *Teachings from the American Earth: Indian Religion and Philosophy* (New York: Liveright, 1975); Walter Capps, ed., *Seeing With a Native Eye: Essays in Native American Religion* (New York: Harper & Row, 1976); Barbara Myerhoff, *Peyote Hunt: The Sacred Journey of the Huichol Indians* (Ithaca, NY: Cornell University Press, 1974).

For the section of African religions, I have regularly assigned Chinua Achebe's novel *Things Fall Apart*. Pedagogically, it serves a function analogous to what *Black Elk Speaks* does as autobiography: make the unfamiliar familiar, render the alien accessible. The story genre in both cases—whether as autobiography or as novel—gives insight into the lives of concrete, individual persons and thereby begins to generate the kinds of questions that scholarly studies address. After reading Achebe we have turned to Benjamin C. Ray, *African Religions: Symbol, Ritual, and Community* (Englewood Cliffs, NJ: Prentice-Hall, 1976) or John S. Mbiti, *African Religions and Philosophy* (New York: Praeger, 1969), or Marcel Griaule, *Conversations with Ogotemmeli* (New York: Oxford University Press, 1965). Robert Cameron Mitchell's *African Primal Religions* (Niles, IL: Argus, 1977) failed to sufficiently challenge my students. I have not yet tried *Beyond "The Primitive": The Religions of Nonliterate Peoples* by Sam Gill (Englewood Cliffs, NJ: Prentice-Hall, 1982) which invites attention.

2

FEMINISM AND WORLD RELIGIONS
Denise Lardner Carmody

There are several ways in which teachers might introduce feminist studies into the mainstream of world religions. Perhaps the best way to proceed would be for me to sketch my own teaching efforts (which have criss-crossed the world religions and Christianity), so that the reader will have one fairly full model against which to react. I apologize for the self-advertising this will entail.

I began with a dual focus. On the one hand, I was asked to teach a course on "Women and Religion" that would serve a developing Women's Studies program (first at Penn State, then at Wichita State). The program was composed of various "Women and . . ." courses: "Women and Business," "Women and the Law," "The Psychology of Women," "The Sociology of Women," etc. On the other hand, I was asked to represent feminist scholarship and feminist interests within my home-base departments of Religious Studies. This meant cross-listing the course on "Women and Religion" as a Religious Studies elective, but also providing for feminist issues in other, usually general courses, such as "Introduction to Religion," "Christianity," "Traditional Religion in the Modern World," and the like.

For the course on "Women and Religion" I developed some historical materials that eventually got condensed into my small book *Women & World Religions* (Nashville: Abingdon, 1979). This is largely a historical overview of the whole, with all the limitations one can imagine in such a venture. Nonetheless, it provides the core information on women's status and image in archaic religions, the religions of India, East Asian religions, Judaism, Christianity, and Islam. In teaching "Women and Religion" I tend to supplement this text with books that give more detail on particular parts of the overall story, with illustrative novels, and with contemporary works that focus on issues of philosophy or spirituality (see below for some of these materials).

When it happened that my husband John and I wrote a textbook on world religions (*Ways to the Center: An Introduction to World Religions*

Denise Lardner Carmody, after several years at Wichita State University, will begin chairing the Religion Faculty at the University of Tulsa (Tulsa, OK 74101) in the 1985 school year. An Associate Editor of Horizons, *she received her doctorate from Boston College in 1970. The most recent of her many books is* Seizing the Apple *(New York: Crossroad, 1984).*

[Belmont, CA: Wadsworth, 1981]), I found myself with an opportunity to represent feminist interests in a new way. We had decided that we wanted our text to combine historical treatments of the major traditions with what we called "structural analyses," and that the latter would have the recurring format (from Eric Voegelin) of nature, society, the self, and divinity. "Society" seemed the best place to consider how the tradition in question had regarded women, though on occasion historical questions also begged attention. In this case, then, we have woven feminist issues into the general story of the world religions, which in turn we take as so many ways to the center of human experience—to the still point of the turning world, if one can bear to have it put poetically. We assume that women have shared the general quest of their culture for such centering (or transcendence, or salvation, or finding meaning), but that the conditions under which they have sought the center have been peculiar enough to warrant our stepping back regularly and noting such conditions. Thus we underscore the Hindu tendency to think that one can only gain *moksha* as a man, the Christian biblical notion that woman is the "weaker vessel," and like colorings of the other traditions' religious quests.

Somewhat similarly, I have gone out of my way to use materials bearing on women's religious experience in a little work entitled *What Are They Saying About Non-Christian Faith?* (Ramsey, NJ: Paulist, 1982). This book surveys recent presentations on archaic, Indian, East Asian, Muslim, and Jewish faith by Christian theologians or Western religious studies scholars. In illustrating Indian materials, for example, I had a variety of options and deliberately decided that some of the studies in Nancy Falk and Rita Gross's *Unspóken Worlds: Women's Religious Lives in Non-Western Cultures* (San Francisco: Harper & Row, 1980) could serve just as well as studies that paid no special attention to women. The conviction behind this decision was that women tend to be the neglected half of the religious population, so that when an opportunity arises to treat commonly human topics through foci on women's experience, taking that opportunity likely will redress the general imbalance at least a little bit.

In my other teaching and writing, where the focus has not been the full span of the world religions but a particular tradition, I have tried to make women's experience either a distinct unit or one of the central threads. So, for example, in my course on archaic religion ("Primitive Religion," "The Religions of Non-Literate People," or whatever other title one prefers), I have tried to make sure that women's rites of passage, economic activities of gathering and farming, association with blood taboos, representation through androgynous divinities or sacred marriages, and the like get enough attention to evoke women's distinctive participation in the general religious patterns of the prehistoric, early civilizational, and recent shamanic religions. My book *The Oldest God* (Nashville: Abingdon, 1981) puts these efforts between covers.

In my course on Christianity, I have tended to concentrate more on recent feminist theological interests than on historical questions, though of course the two naturally go together. This concentration is reflected in the major treatments of feminist issues in the text on Christianity that my husband and I have written (*Christianity: An Introduction* [Belmont, CA: Wadsworth, 1982]). There feminist topics emerge most strongly in Part Three, which deals with recent trends, and next most strongly in Part One, which deals with the Christian world view. (Part Two deals with a historical overview.)

In my course on Catholicism, the motif again has been more topical than historical. This no doubt reflects the emphasis of my own graduate training, for certainly one could stress the historical rather than the topical or systematic. Nonetheless, I have been most interested in recent theological reassessments, and (therefore?) have found them the easiest materials to use for gaining students' interest. Thus I have used Mary Gordon's novels *Final Payments* (New York: Random House, 1978) and *The Company of Women* (New York: Random House, 1980) rather than a work of Juliana of Norwich or Teresa of Avila. Our *Contemporary Catholic Theology: An Introduction* (San Francisco: Harper & Row, 1980) deals with feminism in the context of ecclesiology, suggesting that women's oppression is one of current Catholicism's biggest credibility gaps.

Last, I have put together a "dialogue" or "conversation" between Christian theology and feminism, aimed at the middle ground between extremists (whom I would define as those who feel the other camp has nothing of value to say to them) on both sides. This book (*Feminism and Christianity: A Two-Way Reflection* [Nashville: Abingdon, 1982]), reflects my dual academic citizenship as a member of both Religious Studies Departments and Women's Studies Programs, but it reflects even more my efforts to harmonize the feminist and (Christian) religious parts of my own psyche. I see it as an exercise in what a disciple of Bernard Lonergan might call "communications," and I have been using its materials in talks to Christian church groups, talks to women's groups such as the local chapter of N.O.W., and in such courses as "Women and Religion" and "Christianity."

Before proceeding to a core bibliography that will offer a small indication of the resources available for upping the quotient of feminist materials in general courses, let me indicate some of the generalist work of other writers on whom I have been drawing. *Unspoken Worlds*, already mentioned, covers the full swath of the traditions, with the exception of Judaism and Christianity. (In these two cases, as the editors rightly point out, abundant materials already exist). The advantage of this book is that the anthropological focus of many of the contributors enables them to render the "feel" of the religious tradition as it actually works out for its women. A majority of the studies deal with the recent period and derive from personal interviews. I especially like Charles S. J. White's study, "Mother Guru: Jnanananda of Madras, India," because it allows a powerful, indeed authoritative Indian woman's personality to emerge. James M. Freeman's chapter, "The Ladies of Lord Krishna: Rituals of Middle-Aged Women in Eastern India," takes the notion of *bhakti* off the scholar's shelf to invest it with color and warmth, while Erika Friedl's study, "Islam and Tribal Women in a Village in Iran," follows closely the actual treatment Shiite women have been receiving recently in a representative rural community. Many of the other studies also are fine, and the only criticism I would make of the book as a whole is that the editors might have structured it more clearly. However, its general principle of trying wherever possible to allow women to speak for themselves is commendable.

Rita Gross, one of the two editors of *Unspoken Worlds*, has also edited *Beyond Androcentrism* (Missoula, MT: Scholars Press, 1977), a collection of somewhat disparate essays that illustrate the detailed historical and methodological work feminist scholars have been producing in religion for well over fifty years. I have found Gael Hodgkins' study of Sedna, an Eskimo Goddess, and Joanna Rodgers Macy's study of the Prajnaparamita as the Mother of all Buddhas, especially useful. Arvind Sharma of the University of Sidney, Australia, has plans to edit a book entitled *Women in World Religion* (Queensland, Aust.: University of Queensland Press/Prentice Hall, 1983). The book will gather chapters on the major traditions by specialists in each, and the tentative roster is a minor Who's Who of feminist scholarship in world religions: Diana Paul will do Buddhism, Alaka Hejib will do Hinduism, Priscilla Ching Chung and Julia Ching will do Confucianism and Taoism, Rosemary Ruether will do Christianity, Jane Smith will do Islam, and Rita Gross will do Tribal Societies. I will do Judaism (because Judith Plaskow had to withdraw).

Before turning to works on specific traditions, as contrasted with these works that do most of the whole, I feel I should mention several books that promote feminism itself as a religion. One of them draws on several of the world religions, while the others are more limited in focus, but all of them depart from the traditional context of "world religion," in which a woman's sex was not taken to be a more primary determinant of her world view than was the religious tradition and culture she shared with her male contemporaries.

The most ambitious of these works is Mary Daly's *Gyn/Ecology: The Metaethics of Radical Feminism* (Boston: Beacon, 1978). Its interest to the world religionist lies in its middle section, which details brutalities to women fostered (or at least sanctioned) by Hinduism (suttee), Chinese religion (footbinding), African religions (genital mutilation), Christianity (witchburning) and American medicine (gynecological abuses). This is the negative moment, polar to Daly's positive moments, when she attempts to express a new feminist vision, value-system, and language. I am put off by the rhetoric (indeed, I find it sexist, and so immoral), but I am impressed by the case studies of what women have suffered at the hands of representative religious traditions.

Naomi Goldenberg's *Changing of the Gods* (Boston: Beacon, 1979) has a strong negative moment, in which it argues that Judaism and Christianity will wither away because of the feminist assault on patriarchalism. Positively, it uses Jungian psychology and some aspects of the new witchcraft to project a religion (a psychology, some would say) that could give women sustenance the biblical traditions have withheld. Starhawk (Miriam Simos) is a witch who has written a poetic manual for the rebirth of the ancient traditions of the Great Goddess (*The Spiral Dance* [San Francisco: Harper & Row, 1979]). Celtic sources figure prominently, and the various exercises show great imaginative skill. *The Spiral Dance* also proves more vividly than any analytic essay could how "ecological" the feminist witchcraft can be. The Goddess is in many ways Mother Earth or Mother Nature (and for Starhawk she is not limited to women).

Carol Christ, finally, has written a study of modern feminist literary works that in effect sketches the broad outlines of a new feminist religion. This book, *Diving Deep and Surfacing: Women Writers on Spiritual Quest* (Boston: Beacon, 1980), falls in the genre of "Religion and Literature," and its cultural orbit is limited to the modern West. Nonetheless, its concern with nature, with mystical or peak experiences, and with wholeness, as well as its compatibility with Christ's subsequent focus on the Goddess, merit one's considering it a feminist "Way to the Center"—a feminist programme, inchoate but powerful, for "salvation."

Core Bibliography

Having indicated my own attempts to put feminist factors into the main stream, several generalist works, and several works that present feminism itself as a religion, let me now indicate some sources that I have found helpful for particular aspects of the "world religions" span.

Katherine K. Young and Arvind Sharma have published a bibliography on Women in India (*Images of the Feminine* [Chico, CA: New Horizons, 1974]) that deals with the Buddhist, Hindu, and Islamic traditions. They have also published an outline of their course, "Images of the Feminine in India," (Sydney, Aust.: The University of Sydney Press, 1980).

I. B. Horner's *Women Under Primitive Buddhism* (New York: Dutton, 1930), continues to be useful for the early Pali Literature, while Diana Paul's *Women in Buddhism* (Berkeley: Lancaster-Miller, 1980) treats this tradition with modern critical tools. One can glean many useful notions from A. L. Basham's *The Wonder that Was India* (New York: Grove Press, 1954), because it is wonderfully rich in cultural detail. Stephan Beyer's *The Cult of Tara* (University of California, 1973) deals with a major goddess of Tibetan Buddhism. Sulamith Heinz Potter's *Family Life in a Northern Thai Village: A Study in the Structural Significance of Women* (Berkeley: University of California, 1977) is a good example of the useful studies one can find by browsing the anthropological literature.

Margery Wolf and Roxane Witke have edited a fine volume of anthropological studies on Chinese women (*Women in Chinese Society* [Stanford, CA: Stanford University Press, 1975]), while Elisabeth Croll's *The Women's Movement in China* (London: Anglo-Chinese Educational Institute, 1974) deals with the Maoist innovations. Ichiro Hori's *Folk Religion in Japan* (Chicago: University of Chicago, 1968) has fine materials on Japanese shamanesses. H. Byron Earhart's bibliography on the new religions in Japan (many of them started by women), *The New Religions of Japan: A Bibliography of Western-Language Materials* (Tokyo: Sophia University, 1970) also has many valuable leads.

For Islam, Jane Smith has recently published *Women in Contemporary Muslim Society* (Lewisburg, PA: Bucknell University Press, 1980), and the first-person narratives of *Middle Eastern Women Speak*, edited by Fernea and Bezirgan (Austin, TX: University of Texas Press, 1977), are a rich storehouse. *The Jewish Woman: New Perspectives*, edited by Elizabeth Koltun (New York: Schocken, 1976), has articles dealing with both the present and the past. *Womanspirit Rising*, edited by Carol Christ and Judith Plaskow (San Francisco: Harper & Row, 1979) has studies of Jewish women's current revisionism. Leonard Swidler's *Women in Judaism* (Metuchen, NJ: Scarecrow, 1976) is good on the intertestamental period, and I found Samuel Heilman's *Synagogue Life* (Chicago: University of Chicago Press, 1976) fascinating when read between the lines.

I will not comment on the spate of sources for Christianity, other than to thank Rosemary Ruether for her prodigious labors, both historical and systematic. An area I find especially exciting is archaic religion, in part because so much of the new, radical feminist religion connects to archaic religion through ecology and the Goddess. General works in this area include Carol MacCormack and Marilyn Strathern, *Nature, Culture and Gender* (New York: Cambridge University Press, 1980); Peggy Reeves Sanday, *Female Power and Male Dominance* (New York: Cambridge University Press, 1981), and Michele Rosaldo and Louise

Lamphere, *Woman, Culture & Society* (Stanford, CA: Stanford University Press, 1974). Denise Paulme's *Women of Tropical Africa* (Berkeley: University of California, 1963) collects specialized studies on one geographic area.

Articles

Supplementary studies that I have found useful include Carol P. MacCormack, "Biological Events and Cultural Control," *Signs* (Autumn, 1977); Nancy Falk, "An Image of Woman in Old Buddhist Literature: The Daughters of Mara," in *Women and Religion*, rev. edition, ed. Plaskow and Romero (Scholars Press, 1974); Stella Kramrisch, "The Indian Great Goddess," *History of Religions* (May 1975); Susan Wadley, "Women in the Hindu Tradition," *Signs* (Autumn 1977); Ellen Marie Chen, "Tao as the Great Mother and the Influence of Motherly Love in the Shaping of Chinese Philosophy," *History of Religions* (August 1974); Denise Lardner Carmody, "Taoism and Feminism," *Religion in Life* (Summer 1977); Johannes Maringer, "Clay Figurines of the Jomon Period," *History of Religions* (November 1974); Judith Hauptmann, "Images of Women in the Talmud," *Religion and Sexism*, ed. Rosemary Ruether (Simon & Schuster, 1974); Jacob Neusner, "Thematic or Systematic Description: The Case of Mishnah's Division of Women," in his *Method and Meaning in Ancient Judaism* (Scholars Press, 1979); Chana Poupko and Devora Wohlgelernter, "Women's Liberation: An Orthodox Response," *Tradition* (1976); Jane Smith and Yvonne Haddad, "Women in the Afterlife: The Islamic View as Seen from Qur'an and Tradition," *Journal of the American Academy of Religion* (March 1975); Fatima Mernissi, "Women, Saints, and Sanctuaries," *Signs* (Autumn 1977); Joseph Graziani, "The Status of Women in the Contemporary Muslim Arab Family," *Middle East Review* (Winter 1976-77); and Rita Gross, "Menstruation and Childbirth as Ritual and Religious Experience in the Religion of the Australian Aborigines," *Journal of the American Academy of Religion* (December 1977).

Topics Suitable for Research Papers

Prehistoric Representations of the Fertile Female; The Correlation of Mother Earth and the Female Role in Early Agriculture; Androgyny in the Indian Pantheon; Maternal Imagery for the Cosmis Buddha (*Tathagata-Garba*); The Negative Image of Woman in Indian Tradition; Blood Taboos in Traditional Chinese Religion; Confucian Misogynism; Positive Images of the Feminine in the Taoist Tradition; The Resistance of Japanese Cultural Traditions to Women's Liberation; The Japanese Tradition of Female Shamans; Female Rites of Passage in Non-Literate Peoples (American Indians, Africans, or Australians); Female Saints in

Muslim Tradition; Why Are There More Muslim Women in the Fire than in the Garden?; Purdah and the Harem; Menstrual Taboos in Jewish Tradition; Why Have Jewish Women Been Discouraged from Rabbinic Studies?; The Rise of Women's Ceremonies among Jewish Feminists; Beyond Androcentrism in the History of Religions; Women as Religious Authority Figures (e.g., Gurus); Towards the Feminist Reconstruction of "God"; Is the New Witchcraft a Reversion to Mythic Consciousness?; Sexual Equality as a Sign of the Kingdom of God; Feminism and *Ahimsa* (Non-Violence); Feminism and *Wu-Wei* (Not-Doing); Polanyi's Tacit Dimension and Feminist Methodology in Religious Studies; Does Buddhist Enlightenment Dissolve Sexual Antagonisms?; Nuptial Imagery in Christian Infused Contemplation; and Ecology, Feminism, and Archaic Religious Consciousness.

Books Suitable for Book Reports

Sometimes students can profit from reading with a feminist eye books that take a general theme across the world religions. A good example is Geoffrey Parrinder's *Sex in the World's Religions* (New York: Oxford University Press, 1980). Books that survey daily life in a given period can be read similarly—i.e., be pressed by feminine interests to reveal more than they may intend. Good examples are Jacques Gernet's *Daily Life in China* (Stanford, CA: Stanford University Press, 1970) and Jonathan Spence's *Emperor of China* (New York: Knopf, 1974). Studies that correlate male and female divinities can stimulate interesting theological reflections. See, for example, David Kinsley's *The Sword and the Flute* (Berkeley: University of California Press, 1975) on Kali and Krishna. I have found Robert and Jane Coles's *Women of Crisis* I and II (New York: Delta, 1978 and 1980) useful for the current American situation, because so many of the women interviewed indicate religious sources of sustenance (note especially the Eskimo woman, Lorna, in I).

A number of novels have proven stimulating to my students. Margaret Atwood's *Surfacing* (New York: Popular Library, 1976) expresses the current feminist gravitation toward naturalist religious experience. Kamala Markandaya's *Nectar in a Sieve* (New York: Signet, 1954) sketches poignantly a traditional rural Indian woman's lot. Maxine Hong Kingston's *The Woman Warrior* (New York: Knopf, 1977) and *China Men* (New York: Knopf, 1980) bring old world values to a new feminist psyche with pyrotechnic results. The novels of Yasunari Kawabata are lovely evocations of traditional Japanese culture that say much obliquely about women. See, for example, *Beauty and Sadness* (Rutland, VT: Tuttle, 1975). Ernest Callenbach's *Ecotopia* (New York: Bantam, 1977) includes feminist demands on its futuristic ecological agenda, correlating these demands with a naturalistic worship. Doris Lessings' *The Marriages Between Zones Three, Four, and Five* (New York:

Knopf, 1980) is so rich on androgyny that it can stimulate good discussions of maleness and femaleness in God. Patrick White's *The Eye of the Storm* (New York: Avon, 1975) provocatively sets the life cycle of a white Australian woman on mystical tracks. Last, two novels about prehistoric humanity, Jean Auel's *The Clan of the Cave Bear* (New York: Bantam, 1981) and Bjorn Kurten's *Dance of the Tiger* (New York: Berkeley, 1981), shed light on the earliest women's religious experience.

Last, I find that vivid anthropological studies can seduce students positively. Thus I especially like Colin Turnbull's *The Forest People* (New York: Simon and Schuster, 1962) and *The Mountain People* (New York: Simon and Schuster, 1972), which both include materials on African tribal women. Marcel Griaule's *Conversations with Ogotemmeli* (New York: Oxford University Press, 1965) suggests what the place of the feminine has been in the Dogon religious world. Ruth Underhill's *Red Man's Religion* (Chicago: University of Chicago Press, 1965) includes materials on Indian women. Napoleon Chagnon's *Yanomamo* (New York: Holt, Rinehart, Winston, 1968) treats passingly of women's place in this violent South American tribe. Lastly, one can glean two good collections of myths and stories for primary source on women's lot. These are Mircea Eliade's *From Primitives to Zen* (New York: Harper & Row, 1967) and Barbara Sproul's *Primal Myths* (San Francisco: Harper & Row, 1979).

Evaluations of Current Texts

As far as I am aware, at present (December 1981) the only general text that deals systematically with women in the world religions is our *Ways to the Center*. However, *Religions of the World*, edited by Niels Nielsen (New York: St. Martin's, 1982) has been announced as featuring "careful attention to the inclusion of women's roles and perspectives and to the use of non-sexist language." Of course, new editions of such otherwise useful works as Robert Ellwood's *Many Peoples, Many Faiths* (Englewood Cliffs, NJ: Prentice Hall, 1976), John Noss's *Man's Religions* (New York: Macmillan, 1974), Richard Comstock *et al.*'s *Religion and Man* (New York: Harper & Row, 1971), Ismael Faruqi and David Sopher's *Historical Atlas of the Religions of the World* (New York: Macmillan, 1974), Lewis Hopfe's *Religions of the World* (Encino, CA: Glencoe, 1976), Roger Schmidt's *Exploring Religion* (Belmont, CA: Wadsworth, 1980), John Hutchison's *Paths of Faith* (New York: McGraw-Hill, 1975), Ninian Smart's *The Religious Experience of Mankind* (New York: Scribner's, 1968), and Ward Fellow's *Religions East and West* (New York: Holt, Rinehart, Winston, 1979) may be hit by the new-fangled notion that women are more than half the religious population and so make systematic provision for women's distinctive experience. I pray that the same *metanoia* may afflict such series as

Wadsworth's *The Religious Life of Man*, Argus's *Major World Religions*, and Barron's *Compact Studies of World Religions*, so that one day soon the world's religious women may find in them a voluminous room of their own.

Summary

Briefly, let me boil all this bibliography and opinionated suggestion down to (1) a sketch of a core course, and (2) an estimate of what it will take to get women's experience into the mainstream of the study of world religions. (1) Students can get a core course by working through such few books as Nancy Falk and Rita Gross's *Unspoken Worlds*, Rosemary Ruether's *Religion and Sexism* (or Carol Christ and Judith Plaskow's *Womanspirit Rising*) and Margaret Atwood's *Surfacing* (and/or Maxine Kingston's *The Woman Warrior*). Such a course would touch all the world religious traditions (though somewhat episodically), would offer at least a bow to archaic themes, and would offer one or two novelistic foci for color and interest.

(2) In my opinion, to get women's experience into the mainstream of the study of world religions will take a sort of "affirmative action." By this I mean a temporary bias in favor of things distinctly feminist. To assure that women's rituals, images, access to religious authority, representation in the pantheon, relation to nature, relation to culture, religious value as parents, and the like get treatment equal to men's, we will have to go out of our way to use feminist materials. Further, since many of these materials will reveal that women traditionally have received negative treatment or imaging, this affirmative action will also likely entail a venture in reconstructive theology—an effort to imagine how the future realistically may improve on the past. In my view, the key symbol in such an imaginative effort is the two pans of justice perfectly balanced. As a result, I see both anti-female and anti-male biases as large evils. Women will enter the mainstream of the humanistic profit religious studies courses can generate when they become just as sacred as men.

Additional Bibliography

Christine Downing, *The Goddess* (New York: Crossroad, 1981); Carl Olsen, ed., *The Book of the Goddess* (New York: Crossroad, 1983); Diane Wolksein and Samuel Noah Kramer, *Inanna: Queen of Heaven and Earth* (San Francisco: Harper & Row, 1983).

3

TO SET THE RECORD STRAIGHT: BIBLICAL WOMEN'S STUDIES

Elisabeth Schüssler Fiorenza

In the early 1970's women's studies emerged as an independent discipline. In all areas of scientific knowledge courses and research projects were developed to expand our knowledge of women's cultural-scientific contributions as well as to challenge androcentric texts, scholarly frameworks, and scientific reconstructions that overlooked or marginalized women. Women's studies in religion participate in these intellectual and educational goals of the Women's Studies movement, while feminist theology and feminist studies in religion share in the liberative goals of the feminist movement in society and church. In the context of this two-fold movement, feminist Biblical studies have moved from the concentration on what men have said about women in the Bible and from the apologetic-thematic focus on "women in the Bible" to a new critical reading of Biblical texts in a feminist theological perspective. In this process we have moved from discussing statements of Paul or the "Fathers" and Rabbis about women to the rediscovery of Biblical women's leadership and oppression as crucial for the revelatory process of God's liberation reflected in the Jewish and Christian Scriptures.

In the past decade or so I have regularly taught an undergraduate course on "wo/men in the Bible" that seeks to integrate historical-critical Biblical scholarship, the intellectual women's studies approach, and feminist-theological concerns. Over the years, this course has evolved three basic sections which could easily be taught as separate courses or be integrated as a whole or in part into other Biblical studies, religious studies, or women's studies courses. The course presupposes that students have had an introductory course in theology and that both women and men are enrolled in the class. Although the title announces that the course will discuss the whole Bible I have come to realize that this is an impossible undertaking within the context of a single course, especially if students have no skills in historical-critical analysis and lack basic historical knowledge about Biblical times and situations.

Elisabeth Schüssler Fiorenza, Department of Theology, University of Notre Dame (Notre Dame, IN 46556), is presently Talbot Professor of New Testament at the Episcopal Divinity School (Cambridge, MA 02138). Among her many writings are In Memory of Her (New York: Crossroad, 1983), Bread Not Stone (Boston: Beacon, 1984), and Claiming the Center (Minneapolis, MN: Seabury, 1985). She is an Associate Editor of Horizons.

Since my own area of specialization is New Testament Studies I tend to discuss Old Testament and "patristic" texts only selectively and to concentrate on New Testament texts. However, I suggest that my methodological approach can be employed equally well in the discussion of Old Testament texts and early church writings.

It is obviously impossible to give even a detailed course syllabus and description in such a limited space. What I will try to do, therefore, is sketch the main sections of the course, make some suggestions for student learning processes and assignments, and mention some books which I have found helpful in teaching the course. Since I cannot develop here fully the theological rational and exegetical content of each section, I refer those interested in a fuller theoretical development to my book *In Memory of Her: A Feminist Theological Reconstruction of Christian Origins* (New York: Crossroad, 1983). I am also in the process of developing a student reader that will provide texts and translations not readily available for such a course. Helpful general introductions are also Letty Russell, ed., *The Liberating World* (Philadelphia: Westminster, 1976) and the papers of the 1980 Society of Biblical Literature panel on *The Effects of Women's Studies on Biblical Studies* which were edited by Phyllis Trible and appeared in the *Journal for the Study of the Old Testament* 22 (1982), 3-71.

The bibliography suggested is neither comprehensive nor paradigmatic. I simply mention the books and collections of essays which I have found helpful in preparing and teaching the course. The past decade has produced numerous articles and popular books on "women in the Bible," but the available literature is very uneven in its scholarly quality and theological outlook. For a comprehensive bibliographical review essay see Ross Kraemer, "Women in the Religions of the Greco-Roman World" which will appear in *Religious Studies Review* in 1983.

Issues in Biblical Interpretation

Despite introductory level courses students often have not acquired sufficient skills to read the Bible historically nor have they learned to articulate theological-critical questions with respect to Biblical texts. They usually approach Scripture with a literalist understanding of inspiration and with very little knowledge of the historical world of the Bible or the literary forms and traditions found in it. It is necessary therefore to discuss general introductory questions of Biblical interpretation as well as to explore general feminist theological perspectives before it is possible to introduce specific historical and theological issues. This section therefore addresses (1) the problems of androcentric language, world view, texts, and translations; (2) the question of who wrote Biblical books and why they were written; (3) problems of contemporary interpretation, androcentric presuppositions, models, and prejudices; and (4) questions of Biblical resources and historical reconstructions. This whole introductory section or parts of it can also be taught as segments of general introductory Bible courses, as elements in general courses on religion/theology, and as sections in "women in religion or Christianity" courses. Naturally these segments should also have a place in such specialized Scripture courses or seminars as the Pentateuch, the Prophets, the Pauline letters or the Gospels, or church history.

(1) Since Biblical studies are concerned with the revelatory "word" it is necessary to look carefully at the functions and distortions of androcentric language and male biased translations. While some students might have been alerted to sex-inclusive language either in high-school or earlier college classes, in my experience most students are not conscious of the problem.

The use of "reverse language" is helpful here in raising consciousness. Throughout a whole class period, for example, I will use woman (instead of man) in a generic/inclusive way, use the pronoun she instead of he, and speak about the "boys" on the faculty or in the administration. Since such an exercise will stir a lot of emotions, it is necessary to spend the last part of the class in articulating and discussing such emotions. Another helpful exercise is to read first an androcentric translation of a Biblical text such as a psalm, and then to read the same text in an inclusive form of translation using women and men, she and he, sisters and brothers, God and Godself. Another class period will be spent in a discussion of male biased translation and the reasons for it. It is very helpful to compare four or five different translations of passages such as Gn 1:27; Jer 31:15-22; 1 Cor 11:3 or Rom 16:1. A further question to be explored here is the textual critical question of how our original text was established. Examples are: Rom 16:7, and the identification of "Junian" as a male or female name, or Col 4:15 and its variant readings of "Nympha and the church in her house."

The discussion of these texts can show how androcentric mind-sets and traditions influence the determination and definition of the original text. Do grammatically masculine words such as brothers, saints, elect, apostles, deacons, or elders refer only to men or also to women? What inferences are made in the process of translation? Check the translations of the pronouns for the Holy Spirit in the Bible: Do scholars refer to Her in the Old Testament and to It in the New Testament? How do they translate the term and on the basis of which language? I realize that such exercises require at least some rudimentary knowledge of the Biblical languages on the part of the instructor. However I have found that students can become passionately involved in such questions, and their exploration of these androcentric language issues in a "scientific" manner helps them to question their "literalist" Bible understanding that every word is dictated or inspired by God.

(2) Most helpful in challenging our historical-theological frameworks and assumptions is the question of female authorship of Biblical writings. Traditionally all Biblical books are believed to be written by male authors, although most of the Biblical writings are anonymous or pseudonymous. Such an assumption of female authorship is supported by the suggestions of scholars that a woman could have written, for example, the "Song of Songs" (Trible), Mark (Achtemeier), Proto-Luke (Swidler), John (Schneiders) or Hebrews (Harnack). However such suggestions often presuppose a "feminine" style, experience, or sensibility which is difficult to establish. Nevertheless such suggestions of female authorship bring to consciousness our unreflected bias that only males could formulate holy Scripture and could claim the authority to do so.

Moreover, the assumption of female authorship also has great value in engendering a different historical imagination. For instance, I find very helpful the creative exercise of writing "apostolic" letters to be attributed to Old Testament or early Christian women leaders. Students can write, for example, an announcement of Deborah to the people of Israel, a letter of Phoebe to the community at Cenchreae, a sermon of the apostle Junia addressed to the church of Jerusalem, or a letter of the missionary Prisca to the church of Ephesus. Such letter writing requires students to discuss the form of the letter in antiquity, the situation of the recipients, the motives of the author, and the social-religious context of the time.

(3) This discussion will lead the class into explorations of contemporary interpretations and their presuppositions and prejudices. One can compare different scholarly interpretations of Biblical texts on women and their presuppositions or implications. Another valuable exercise is role playing. For example, choose Ex 1:12-2:10; The birth of Moses and his adoption by Pharaoh's daughter. Read the text aloud and have the whole class identify the main characters of the text; then break into smaller groups, each choosing one character to be discussed and impersonated. The smaller groups discuss the event, clarify historical questions, and imagine the scene by speaking in the first person: "I the midwife or the daughter of the Pharaoh thought, feared, hoped, etc." When the whole class comes together again, the small groups stay together and engage as "group-persons" in a dialogue, raising questions, expressing their feelings in the situation, and acting out the story. At the end, take fifteen minutes to evaluate the role play and its assumptions with the whole class: Discuss the issues which remained open, elaborate historical aspects, and reflect on the attitudes, emotions, and insights generated by the role play. What kind of assumptions were made about the midwife, the mother of Moses, the daughter of Pharaoh, or God?

Among other texts which lend themselves to such role play and the exploration of presuppositions, attitudes, and feelings are Hos 1-4 (Hosea and Gomer); Gn 29-31 (Leah, Rachel, and Bilhah); Mk 7:34-40 (the Syrophoenician Woman); and Acts 12:12-17. It is important, however, to alert students not only to anti-woman biases but also to class, race or anti-Jewish assumptions, which color their role interaction and come to the fore in the role play. Another suggestion: listen to "Jesus Christ Superstar" and see how Mary Magdalen is portrayed, or discuss the liturgical readings for her feastday in different lectionaries.

(4) Not only contemporary interpretations but also Scriptural writings themselves reflect an androcentric world view and patriarchal structures. It becomes necessary therefore to speak about tradition and redaction as well as about literary form and purposes of Biblical writings. It is important to elaborate, for example, that Gen 2-3 is an etiological story which seeks to understand the origin of the world and the evil in it. Students must relinquish their preconception that this story is an historical record and accurate description of what happened. Similarly they have to abandon their assumption that Acts gives us a comprehensive and accurate historical description of developments in the beginnings of the church. It is thus helpful to compare the references of the Pauline letters to women with those of Acts, or to compare the understandings of apostleship in Paul and Luke-Acts.

Equally helpful is a comparison of the gospel stories on women to see which writer has more stories or how the different gospels picture the leading women and the leading men in the discipleship of Jesus. Also fruitful is a careful comparison of one gospel story found in all four accounts—the woman who anointed Jesus, for example. Walter Wink has suggested a "socratic" method for dialoguing with the gospel texts. However, rather than bringing the woman into a direct dialogue with Jesus or oneself, it is better to let students write a dialogue between the woman and the writer of Luke's gospel, asking him why he portrayed her as he did, why he made her a public sinner, etc. This approach avoids a simplistic historicizing of the text and makes redactional deliberations conscious.

Another possibility is to rewrite the story of Miriam or Jezebel, the prophetess, from the point of view of one of her followers, or to let the women who experienced Jesus' miraculous feeding or the mother of Jairus' daughter tell these stories from their own perspectives. How would one tell the story of the prodigal son from his mother's perspective? What theological implications come to the fore in doing so? Another way to raise questions of tradition and redaction is to divide students into small groups, giving each group the same materials (stories, sayings, songs, prayers, commands, folksayings, reports, advertisements), and asking them to use these materials to compose a letter, a children's-hour, a theological lecture, a commencement speech, or a sermon. At the end discuss why the group selected certain texts and not others, why they established a certain sequence, what their major goals were, whom they addressed and how this determined their choice of materials. Another suggestion: let students collect pictures of the annunciation and discuss the different representations found in different centuries and cultures in order to highlight how every generation or group understands and interprets the same tradition differently.

Bibliographical suggestions: For a general discussion of the interaction between culture, society and the definition of gender roles see Ann Oakley, *Sex, Gender, and Society* (San Francisco: Harper & Row, 1972). See especially Casey Miller and Kate Swift, *Words and Women* (Garden City, NY: Doubleday Anchor, 1977) for the discussion of inclusive language. Suggestions for female Biblical language metaphors are found in Phyllis Trible, *God and the Rhetoric of Sexuality* (Philadelphia: Fortress, 1978). See also her interpretation of Gen 1-3 and the book of Ruth. Interpretations of Gospel stories from a woman's point of view are found in Rachel Conrad Wahlberg, *Jesus According to a Woman* (New York: Paulist, 1975) and *Jesus and the Freed Woman* (New York: Paulist, 1978), whereas Leonard Swidler, *Biblical Affirmations of Woman* (Philadelphia: Westminster, 1979) provides a good overview of all the Biblical texts on women. Elisabeth Moltmann Wendel, *The Women Around Jesus* (New York: Crossroad, 1982) is not only helpful for interpreting the gospel stories about women but also for tracing the tradition of interpretation. A helpful general introduction to feminist theological questions is Carol Christ and Judith Plaskow, eds., *Womanspirit Rising* (San Francisco: Harper & Row, 1979), especially the editors' introduction.

Wo/Men in the Bible

This section seeks to analyze and reinterpret the information on women which we find in Biblical writings. It is important to distinguish clearly between two types of texts. On the one hand we have those texts which inform us about the actual situation and role of Greco-Roman, Jewish, and early Christian women, reminding us that Christian women remained Jews, Asians, Romans, Greeks or Syrians, although they were all defined politically by the Roman empire and culturally by Hellenism. On the other hand we have those texts which express the opinions, judgments or injunctions of men *about* women. Such a distinction is preferable over the widespread differentiation between positive and negative texts or traditions which does not sufficiently reflect on the interaction of these texts and the social-ecclesial struggles reflected in them.

Students must first become conscious of how little they know about the subject matter and of how greatly this knowledge may be tainted by prejudice. When asked to list ten Biblical women, many students, despite extensive religious schooling, are able to mention only Eve and Mary, the Mother of Jesus, and perhaps Mary Magdalene, the whore. Assigned interviews with their friends and other students usually produce similar results. More importantly, many students are ignorant either about Greco-Roman antiquity or about Judaism in antiquity. Yet almost all have picked up the apologetic argument that Christianity has very much improved the status of women, who in Judaism or the Greco-Roman world were supposedly considered to be "chattel," minors, or "immoral."

It is therefore important to make students aware that the first followers of Jesus and Christian missionaries were Jewish and Greco-Roman women who were free to convert and to define their own religious-social commitments. A discussion of the patriarchal structures of the ancient world therefore needs to point out that within the Greco-Roman world of the first century women, especially rich women, had achieved a relative emancipation which often gave them more autonomy and freedom than that of women of the nineteenth century or even today.

An example of an independent Jewish woman is found in the book of Judith, while the excavations of Pompeii, for instance, have documented the economic wealth of some women and the participation even of working women in the public life of the city. The androcentric character of statements made by male authors about women must be analyzed not only in early Christian but also in Jewish and Greco-Roman writings. For example, the satires of Juvenal give us information about the high level of women's education, but at the same time they distort this information because of their misogynist slant. Similarly, Rabbinic statements are not descriptions of women's situation in the first century but rather projections and injunctions which reflect the male centered mind-set of their authors.

The ministry of Jesus and the movement initiated by him must therefore not be reconstructed over and against Judaism but in the awareness that Jesus' vision is nurtured by the emancipatory traditions of Judaism and that his first followers were Jewish women and men. The religion and heritage of Judaism are the inspiration and matrix of the Jesus movement. The same holds true for the early Christian missionary movement, which at first was carried on by Jewish wo/men but then moved beyond the boundaries of Judaism. This movement too was possible only because in the Greco-Roman world there existed groups and associations which were not patterned after the patriarchal structures of the dominant culture.

The reconstruction of the early Christian movements must therefore take into account the relative emancipation of women in the Greco-Roman world as well as chart the relationship of the early Christian movement to its dominant patriarchal culture. The transition from the pre-Pauline to the post-Pauline churches must be carefully analyzed, and the role of Paul in this transition must be pinpointed. Most of the post-Pauline writings are addressed to or located in Asia Minor. The so-called household-code-texts that reintroduce patriarchal values and structures into the Christian movement are all addressed to communities in this area. This is significant, since we know that the status of Asian women was exceptionally high. It needs to be kept in mind when discussing the role of women in Revelations, 1 Peter, the Pastorals, the Johannine Epistles, or Ignatius, that slave women were most negatively affected by the patriarchalization of the church.

In order to place the New Testament writings in their early Christian contexts it is important to discuss what information we have about women of the first Christian centuries and to familiarize students with the Apocryphal Acts, Gnostic writings, Montanist oracles, church orders or "patristic" writers. I have found tests and short papers most helpful in achieving the goal of this section, which is to broaden students' Biblical-historical and theological knowledge. I usually assign certain readings, hand out study questions, ask them to look up words, to draw maps, or to analyze certain texts. Since many of my students do not come from Arts & Letters, but from Business Administration, Architecture, or the Sciences, they usually are better equipped to handle informational questions and "true or false" tests than to write research papers. Some of the more advanced students, however, have written papers on topics such as male and female disciples in the Gospel of Mark; interpretations of Gal 3:28; Women in the Fourth Gospel; comparison between Paul's references to women and those in Acts; the "widow" in the Pastoral epistles; Ephesians 5 in our wedding liturgy; the matriarchs in the Old Testament; women prophets in the Old Testament and New Testament; Ruth and Naomi; women in the Acts of Thecla and Paul; "Should we proclaim patriarchal texts as the 'word of God'?"; marriage legislation in Jewish and Roman law; Isis and her worship; comparison of different creation-stories. However, most students who are not theology majors find such papers are often too complex and discouraging.

Bibliographical Suggestions. J. H. Otwell, *And Sarah Laughed: The Status of Women in the Old Testament* (Philadelphia: Westminster, 1977) and Evelyn and Frank Stagg, *Woman in the World of Jesus* (Philadelphia: Westminster, 1978) discuss a wealth of information, although their tone is sometimes apologetic-defensive. More critical and feminist in outlook are the first six chapters in Rosemary Radford Ruether, ed., *Religion and Sexism* (New York: Simon & Schuster, 1974), while the first two chapters in Rosemary Ruether and Eleanor McLaughlin, eds., *Women of Spirit* (New York: Simon & Schuster, 1979) seek to highlight women's contributions to early Christianity. A concise and useful discussion of women's ministry in early Christianity is Elizabeth M. Tetlow's *Women and Ministry in the New Testament* (New York: Paulist, 1980), although it sometimes simplifies difficult exegetical problems. Information on women in the Greco-Roman world is found in S. B. Pomeroy, *Goddesses, Whores, Wives, and Slaves* (New York: Schocken, 1975) and Mary R. Lefkowitz and Maureen B. Fant, eds., *Women in Greece and Rome* (Toronto: Samuel-Stevens, 1977). B. Brooten, *Women Leaders in the Ancient Synagogue* (Chico, CA: Scholars Press, 1983) corrects the anti-Jewish assumptions found in much of Christian literature on "Women in the Bible." The following are helpful for study of women in various groups of the early Church. P. Wilson-Kastner et al., *A Lost Tradition: Women Writers of the Early Church* (Washington, DC: University Press of America, 1981) discuss the writings of Perpetua, Proba, Egeria, and Eudokia, whereas JeanLaPorte, *The Role of Women in Early Christianity* (New York: Mellen, 1982) has edited texts of the "Fathers" on women. S. L. Davies, *The Revolt of the Widows* (Carbondale: Southern Illinois University Press, 1980) proposes that the apocryphal Acts are written by and for women whereas Elaine Pagels, *The Gnostic Gospels* (New York: Random House, 1979) discusses women and the divine in Gnosticism.

Biblical Theological Issues Today

This section of the course explores the significance and importance of Biblical texts for today. It does so by confronting students with questions directed to the Bible by women's studies in religion or by the feminist movement in church and society. Some students will be aware of such questions as masculine god-language or the ordination of women, others will encounter them for the first time, while a few students might have enrolled in the course because they are wrestling with these theological questions. I usually do not teach this segment of the course as a separate section but either integrate the topics into the lectures of the first two sections or assign group projects. Generally I leave it up to the group as to how they want to explore the topic, to formulate their questions, and to present their insights to the whole class. Naturally this section could be taught as an independent course or could be integrated into other courses of theology or women's studies in religion.

Topics of such group projects include: Are women the image of God? (see Gn 1-3; 1 Cor 11:3 and 1 Tim 2); Christian Discipleship and Patriarchal Marriage; the "independent" woman today and in antiquity; God—the Father or How do you pray?; Is "maleness" constitutive in the New Testament for understanding Jesus Christ?; non-sexist prayers and Bible stories for children; a celebration of Mary Magdalene and other Biblical women; Is the Church patriarchal?; Biblical arguments against the ordination of women; women's ordination in other Christian churches; women in Judaism; Biblical arguments of the Moral Majority for the patriarchal family; contemporary and Biblical attitudes toward menstruation and sexual "purity"; the function of the Bible against slaves' and women's suffrage in the nineteenth century; Mary the Mother of God and the Goddesses of antiquity.

Students have developed creative ways of presenting and exploring the problems and topics. One group which discussed the "image of God" question staged a retrial of Eve in order to adjudicate whether her punishment fit her crime. Since most of the group members intended to go to law school, they carefully followed court protocol. At the end the class voted narrowly that Eve's punishment by far exceeded her crime. Another group followed the model of Judith Plaskow's story "The Coming of Lilith," but retold the Genesis story from an African or Asian perspective. Another group prepared a passover meal and haggadah, while others celebrated a feminist baptismal liturgy. A multi-media show on the Goddess was worked out in cooperation with a professor from the art department. Other groups polled their co-students on questions such as menstruation or inclusive god-language, interviewed parents about non-sexist religious education or interviewed priests and nuns on campus about "religious life." Others visited ministers from other churches for an interview. Some visited a Catholic pentecostal household. Other projects included television shows, e.g., on Divorce and the Church; a counseling session with a couple disagreeing on child-rearing; a role play on the housechurch of Nympha; a radio-interview with the Pope, Sister Theresa Kane, Hans Küng and Phyllis Schlafly on women's ordination. These group projects are usually more interesting when some members are older, married, or members of religious orders. Usually they are the most exciting part of the course since they not only foster theological research skills but also allow students to display their imagination or professional skills. Moreover they bring students together in "teamwork" and often result in friendship groups. Although it is difficult to evaluate these group-events, I would not want to miss them. They allow for a Biblical-historical and feminist-theological integration that cannot be accomplished by the instructor alone.

Bibliographical Suggestions. Walter Burkhardt, ed., *Woman: New Dimensions* (New York: Paulist, 1975); Rosemary Radford Ruether, *Sexism and God-Talk* (Boston: Beacon, 1983); Mary Daly, *Beyond God the Father* (Boston: Beacon, 1973); Carol P. Christ, *Diving Deep and Surfacing* (Boston: Beacon, 1980); Judith Plaskow, *Sex, Sin and Grace* (Washington, DC: University Press of America, 1980); J. Chamberlain Engelsman, *The Feminine Dimension of the Divine* (Philadelphia: Westminster, 1979) "fits" the texts into a Jungian interpretational pattern; Robert Hamerton Kelly, *God the Father* (Philadelphia: Fortress, 1979) is somewhat apologetic; Rosemary Radford Ruether, *The Feminine Face of the Church* (Philadelphia: Westminster, 1977); Raymond E. Brown et al., eds., *Mary in the New Testament* (Philadelphia: Fortress, 1978); Marina Warner, *Alone of All Her Sex* (New York: Knopf, 1976); N. Shange, *For Colored Girls Who Have Considered Suicide . . .* (New York: Macmillan, 1975); Arlene Swidler, *Sistercelebrations* (Philadelphia: Fortress, 1974); Leonard and Arlene Swidler, eds., *Women Priests* (New York: Paulist, 1977); E. Koltun, *The Jewish Woman* (New York: Schocken, 1976); C. F. Parvey, *Ordination of Women in Ecumenical Perspective*, Faith and Order Paper, 105 (Geneva: World Council of Churches, 1980).

Additional Bibliography

Elisabeth Schüssler Fiorenza, *Bread Not Stone: The Challenge of Feminist Biblical Interpretation* (Boston: Beacon, 1984); Letty Russell, ed., *Feminist Interpretation of the Bible* (Philadelphia: Westminster, 1985).

4

RECOVERING WOMEN'S HISTORY: EARLY CHRISTIANITY

Rosemary Rader

As I was about to begin my teaching career at Arizona State University in 1977, I shared with one of my colleagues at another university that I was going to teach a course on women in the Christian tradition. He jokingly responded, "Well, that should take about ten minutes. What are you going to do the rest of the semester?" Accepting what I perceived as a well-intentioned challenge, I have occasionally sent him a syllabus for one of the two courses on women and religion which I regularly teach in alternate semesters. Although continuing research, new publications, and insights gleaned from previous classes demand that I change the courses slightly each semester, a perennial frustration remains: the sixteen-week semester is barely adequate for an in-depth study of relevant reading materials, pertinent issues raised, and questions demanding response.

The two courses I alternately teach are "Women in the Christian Tradition" and "Women, Religion, and Social Change" (World Religions). The first I have taught regularly since my arrival at Arizona State (my area is History of Christianity). The second developed as a consequence of a stimulating and provocative team-teaching effort with Diana Paul at Stanford University where I was invited to teach for Winter and Spring quarters, 1980-81. We team-taught the course, "Women, Religion, and Social Change." Professor Paul's insights regarding women's roles in Buddhism and other non-Western religious traditions have been invaluable in both the structuring and the content of this course which I now teach in alternate semesters. Since Denise Carmody has already dealt with the topic, "Feminism and World Religions" (*Horizons* 9/2 [Fall 1982], 313-22), I shall limit my observations and suggestions to the following: (1) the basic outline and suggested readings for the course, "Women in the Christian Tradition," and (2) the ways in which I incor-

Rosemary Rader is Associate Professor in the History of Christianity in the Religious Studies Department at Arizona State University (Tempe, AZ 85281). She holds the Ph.D. in Religious Studies and Humanities from Stanford University. She has published books and articles on Early Christianity, the most recent of which is Breaking Boundaries: Male/Female Friendship in Early Christian Communities (New York: Paulist, 1983). For several years she has been chair of the Women and Religion section of the Western Regional American Academy of Religion.

porate feminist issues into the two basic courses on the history of Christianity ("Introduction to Christianity" and "Formation of Christian Traditions"). I shall briefly discuss the basic issues studied in the courses and shall list most bibliographical sources at the end of the article.

"Women in the Christian Tradition" deals primarily with the status and roles of women in Christianity, with special emphasis on cultural conditioning and historical developments responsible for the initiation and maintenance of sex-differentiated roles. Indirectly the course serves as an introduction to the study of religion in that it includes readings and discussions on the role of religion in any given culture, the political aspects of religion, and the function and force of language, myths, and symbols in shaping and maintaining sex-differentiated roles.

I introduce the course with a session on the role of religion in shaping an individual or group's responses to the varied experiences of life. I find Mary Gordon's *Final Payments* (New York: Random House, 1978) particularly helpful in that most students in the class can somehow relate to the fact that guilt feelings are often evoked by adherence to certain religious views and beliefs. Selections from Simone de Beauvoir's *The Second Sex* (New York: Random House, 1952) can also be used effectively, though the language and conceptual framework are often a deterrent to clarity of focus. As students begin to question the unequal distribution of guilt and its consequent double standards in society sexism emerges as the culprit. Once the culprit has been identified and defined, the question of religion's role in accepting and even propagating the network of attitudes, behaviors, and norms which result from sex-role stereotyping reemerges. The focus shifts from religions in general to Christianity as the particular focus of our study. Since contemporary evidence indicates that sexism is an integral aspect of the many forms of Christianity, the study leads to an exercise in reconstructing the world of Christian origins in order to explain *how* and *why* sexism became so pervasive within that religion.

Since religion, like culture itself, does not develop from a vacuum, the reconstruction of Christian origins demands at least a cursory study of women in both the Greco-Roman and the Judaic world. Since Chapter Two of my book, *Breaking Boundaries: Male/Female Friendship in Early Christian Communities* (New York: Paulist, 1983) deals with "Normative Greco-Roman and Judaic Male/Female Relationships," I use much of that material to examine women's status and roles in those traditions. Students are generally surprised to learn that women of the first century A.D. had achieved a degree of freedom and autonomy unparalleled in later periods of history. Since most students are not very knowledgeable about women in the various Hellenistic societies and many have stereotypical attitudes about women in Judaism, there is not only the opportunity, but the necessity, to examine *how* one locates and interprets material about women in any given culture. An article which has proved useful in this regard (though it itself calls for some "interpretation," particularly for undergraduates) is Jacob Neusner's "Thematic or Systemic Description: The Case of Mishnah's Division of Women" (*Method and Meaning in Ancient Judaism*, Brown Judaic Studies 10 [Missoula, MT; Scholars Press, 1979], pp. 79-100). Questions which naturally arise from the readings and discussions center on (1) the role of cultural conditioning in a group's self-identification, (2) the lack of correlation between a group's theoretical views on the integrity and worth of individuals and the oppressive, misogynistic treatment of individuals, and (3) the contradiction between the theoretical symbolic glorification of women and the every-day functional, social oppression of women.

In reconstructing the world of male/female relationships and the groups' sex-role systems, students begin to analyze the importance of myths and symbols in defining, maintaining, and/or changing the views, beliefs, and practices of the group(s). The etiological myths of Pandora and Eve are studied and discussed, with particular emphasis on the implications of the stories for establishing negative attitudes about women and legitimating the subjugation of women by men. The students generally perceive how myths are used to propagate the false assumptions resulting from a confusion of what is "natural" with what is "cultural." One of the most effective pedagogical techniques in "exorcising the patriarchal demon" (to borrow Sheila Collins' phrase) is to have the students rewrite a myth and share the revised version with the class. This is usually a highlight of the course in that for the first time many students begin to understand the power of "story" in establishing the value-system of a group. Both the provocative discussions which ensue and the student evaluations at the end of the course indicate the importance of this exercise in understanding part of the process by which misogynistic views and practices were incorporated into societies.

I generally introduce the study of women in early Christianity by having the students read the *Acts of Paul and Thecla*, the *Gospel of Mary*, and excerpts from the *Gospel of Thomas* and the *Gospel of Philip*. Most, if not all, students have never read these works, and their amazement at the instances of non-marginal status of women leads them to question the dictum that Christianity was *always* a man's religion. In reconstructing the various worlds of early Christianity the students are made aware of texts written by women (though few are extant), and of other texts demonstrating that in many areas of early Christianity women were far from being the marginal characters that later androcentric bias posited. The texts are never read in isolation but are set within the context of political and social worlds of their time. Two slight, easily readable volumes which aid the students in understanding the context which allowed for early Christian "liberation movements" are Peter Brown's *The Making of Late Antiquity* (Cambridge: Harvard University Press, 1978), and Tom B. Jones's *In the Twilight of Antiquity* (Minneapolis: University of Minnesota Press, 1978). Both stress the need to evaluate materials from this period within the context of the fluid, transitional age which evoked them. The students begin to see how, within this larger world view, the early Christians could regard Christ as the obliterator of the male/female, slave/free, and Jew/Gentile polarities. An article which deals specifically with this issue and opens up the question of correlation between theological formulation and practical application is Wayne Meeks's "The Image of the Androgyne: Some Uses of a Symbol in Earliest Christianity" (*History of Religions* 13 [February 1974], 165-208). The students question whether the elimination or minimization of sexual inequalities was not part of a larger movement within societies of that time which stressed unity through unification of opposites.

As the students read about the diversity of women's roles in the early Church and the fact that women maintained and even initiated many Christian traditions (e.g., the agape celebration, monastic communities, charitable institutions) they challenge later androcentric interpretations which have minimized or totally obliterated women's roles and experiences in this crucial period of history. The texts I use here are those cited in *Breaking Boundaries*, particularly readings from the New Testament, apocryphal writings, letters, the *Vitae* of women and men, essays, and edicts and decrees which directly or indirectly provide commentary on women's experiences. (I eagerly await Schüssler Fiorenza's student reader.) Questions emerge which lead the students to understand *how* women's history from this period was eventually "lost" or forgotten. The questions involve the issues of text selection, interpretation, and evaluation within a patriarchal culture, the "normative" aspects of canonization of texts, sexual discrimination as by-product of the church's institutionalization, women's leadership roles identified with heretical movements, the tenuous line between heresy and orthodoxy, the role of language in establishing and maintaining superior/inferior dichotomies, and the incontrovertible fact that "the winners write the history." These issues are the *core* of the course and take up approximately one-third of the course-outline. Since I use the historical-critical method in much the same way (and using many of the same texts) as Elisabeth Schüssler Fiorenza describes it in "To Set the Record Straight: Biblical Women's Studies" (*Horizons* 10/1 [Spring 1983], 111-21), I shall not go into detail here, but strongly urge the readers to utilize the valuable suggestions she offers.

After the scrutiny of available materials from early Christianity and a study of the issues listed above, I generally give several summary lectures on women in Western Medieval and Renaissance Christianity, women in the Reformation and post-Reformation era, women in American religious history, and the effects of the contemporary feminist movement on Christian denominations today. Since there is no one text which can adequately deal with such a huge span of history, I place books and articles on reserve which elaborate on or clarify aspects of the lecture topics (see Bibliography below). Although the focus of this article is chiefly on women in early Christianity, let me just add that a brief summary of events dealing with women's roles and status between the sixth to the twentieth century is very important for the student's understanding of the economic, political, and social complexities affecting women's lives today.

The last several sessions of the course (the number of sessions depends upon the size of the class) are devoted to student presentations summarizing the basic content of the paper which is the final requirement of the course. About half-way through the course the students, in consultation with the instructor, choose a suitable paper topic and begin work on a bibliography. To help the students locate materials, the class meets in the library for one session. There Debbie Blouin, the library consultant for Women's Studies, gives the students a lecture on and a guided tour of the library's reference tools related to women and religion, women and history, etc. I strongly recommend that, wherever such service is available, the instructor take advantage of such resources. Each semester as I take another group for this lecture-tour I find that the reference-consultant's expertise and hard work have saved me many hours of searching for recent bibliographical materials. That, plus the fact that students feel free thereafter to consult with Ms. Blouin on their specific paper topics, frees the instructor for other tasks. Each student is allowed 15-20 minutes to summarize his/her paper (though the paper is not yet in its "finished" state) and the rest of the students add their comments, questions, and suggestions. This serves two purposes; it allows the individual student to revamp the paper if the instructor's and other students' comments suggest such, and it adds additional information and insights to that gleaned from the lectures, readings, and discussions. The students' paper topics vary widely, and I encourage them to choose a topic which really interests them and/or is particularly relevant to their own area of study (anthropology, sociology, religious studies, etc.). Since many students in the class are taking the course towards a minor in Women's Studies (officially, a Certificate of Concentration in Women's Studies, twenty-one semester hours) their papers reflect a broader background than one generally finds in papers submitted. The final class session is generally a combination of instructor's summary-lecture of issues raised, and open dialogue on students' evaluation of and suggestions for the course when offered again.

After having taught this course seven times, I would suggest that for both the instructor and the students the most effective time slot is a three-hour session, 1:40-4:30 p.m. once a week. I discovered that one hour three times a week did not allow for adequate discussion, and even the 1-½ hours twice a week usually frustrated the participants when they had to stop just as the discussion gained momentum. The once-a-week three-hour slot also allows working men and women to attend who can more easily arrange to be excused one afternoon rather than two or three times during the week. The format I have found most successful is a one-hour lecture, a ten to fifteen minute break, another fifteen to twenty minute lecture (aimed at provoking discussion) followed by a forty-minute to one hour discussion on lecture and reading materials. I have the option of teaching the course as REL 390 (all undergraduates) or REL 494 (upper class and graduates). The format and content is generally the same though the REL 390 requires fewer readings and a shorter final paper.

My suggestions for incorporating feminist issues into the courses "Introduction to Christianity" and "Formation of Christian Traditions" will necessarily be brief because I "eclipse" materials from those sources listed above. In the "Introduction" course, I aim the study at the varieties of Christianity seen in contemporary society. After a brief chronological accounting of Christianity's (Christianities'?) developments, the course focuses on contemporary issues, one of which is the effects of feminist movements on contemporary Christian denominations. I usually introduce this topic with something that not only evokes dialogue, but, for some of the more evangelically oriented, provokes agitation. Leonard Swidler's "Jesus was a Feminist" (*Catholic World* [January 1971], 177-83), serves as a good introduction in that it is easily comprehensible and introduces the issue of women's roles through close association with Jesus. Another provocative article is Elaine Pagels' "The Gnostic Vision" (*Parabola* 3/4 [November 1978], 6-9), which calls into question the gradual elimination of women's experiences in Christian records. This allows for several lectures on early Christian egalitarian structures and their subsequent demise. In the "Formation" course there is more opportunity to include factual data about women's history since the course deals with the first six hundred years of Christianity. Emphasis is placed on those aspects which were an integral part of the formation of any new group which seeks to establish its self-identification. Students read and discuss canonical and non-canonical sources giving clues to the formation of the world of early Christianity, its origins within the Greco-Roman and Judaic societies, its borrowings and adaptations, in brief, a shorter incorporation of those topics studied at length in the "Women in the Christian Tradition" course. The important part is that students study the materials as an *integrated* and *integral* part of the course. The material is presented as matter-of-factly as is the more generally accepted androcentric material handed down by its patristic authors. The feminist issues are incorporated into every aspect of the study: the myths, symbols, rituals, male-God imagery, leadership models, egalitarian roles, Constantinian politics, expansion of Christian communities, and development of hierarchical structures. The course admirably lends itself to studying history "as it was," and "as it became." Such a study serves as a necessary corrective to the way Christian history has been, and is still being, taught. It has its problems in that not only is there a dearth of extant materials, but many translations of existing materials are still not available. Also, other pedagogical methods need to be tested which allow the materials to define and clarify those issues which impinge on women's experiences. Progress, however, is forthcoming as long as journals such as this include sections on Creative Teaching which allow for ongoing dialogue about course format and content.

Suggested Paper Topics

The topics listed below are titles of some of the more provocative papers written by students in the "Women in the Christian Tradition" courses: The Mary Cult: Its Origins at the Council of Ephesus; Comparative/Contrastive Study of Isis and Mary; Female Saints in Early Christianity; Christian Pilgrimage: Extending Women's Options; the Eva/Ave Syndrome; Pedestal Politics: Restricting Women's Influence and Roles in Early Christianity; Women's Monastic Communities: A Christian Option; Matristics: Christian Women's Writings; Female Imagery in Early Christian Art; Female Imagery in Gnostic Writings; Paul's Letters: Conflicting Views on Women?; The Interpretation of the Genesis Creation Stories in Early Christianity; Thecla and Paul: Fact or Fiction; The Desert Mothers; Androcentric Reshaping of Earliest Christian Traditions; Male/Female Forms of Ministry in Early Christianity; Women Prophets in Early Christian Movements.

Bibliographical Suggestions

Sexism and Gender Roles

Jane Chetwood and Oonagh Hartnett, eds., *The Sex-Role System: Psychological and Sociological Perspectives* (London: Routledge & Kegan Paul, 1978).
Contributions by various authors who trace the phenomenon of sex-role stereotyping through many different disciplines and areas of study. The studies show how presuppositions about male and

female role expectations color people's perceptions and radically affect views and practices.

Lorene Clark and Lynda Lange, eds., *The Sexism of Social and Political Theory: Women and Reproduction from Plato to Nietzsche* (Toronto: University of Toronto Press, 1979).

The authors deal with the way in which woman's being defined by her unique capacity for reproduction has thoughout history justified her relegation to a subordinate position.

Carol MacCormack and Marilyn Strathern, *Nature, Culture and Gender* (New York: Cambridge University Press, 1980).

A basic study of the ways in which all three define and relegate roles within the structure of society.

Alice Schlegel, ed., *Sexual Stratification: A Cross-Cultural View* (New York: Columbia University Press, 1977).

The assumption of a universal male dominance is called into question through fourteen case studies from both traditional and modern societies. Particularly helpful are the authors' assessments of the role ideology plays in establishing norms for sex roles and status.

Carol Smart and Barry Smart, eds., *Women, Sexuality and Social Control* (London: Routledge & Kegan Paul, 1978).

Deals with the many different dimensions of the social control of women, and offers critiques of the ideological and material conditions which control women and perpetuate their oppression.

Role of Myth

Berenice A. Carroll, ed., *Liberating Women's History: Theoretical and Critical Essays* (Chicago: University of Illinois Press, 1976).

Although not geared solely to "myth," these helpful essays discuss method and content for studying many neglected or forgotten aspects of women's history.

Sheila D. Collins, *A Different Heaven and Earth* (Valley Forge, PA: Judson Press, 1974).

Particularly useful for students' understanding of the de-mythologizing/remythologizing process necessary for changing myths within a culture.

Edmund R. Leach, "Genesis as Myth" in *Myth and Cosmos: Readings in Mythology and Symbolism*, ed. John Middleton (Garden City, NY: Natural History Press, 1967), pp. 1-13.

Jonathan Z. Smith, "The Influence of Symbols upon Social Change: A Place on Which to Stand," *Worship* 44/8 (October 1978), 457-74.

A provocative, though brief, study of the way in which symbols and social structures are derived from a people's vision of its place in the cosmos.

Language

Mary Ritchie Key, *Male/Female Language: With a Comprehensive Bibliography* (Metuchen, NJ: Scarecrow Press, 1975).
Robin Lakoff, *Language and Woman's Place* (New York: Harper and Row, 1975).
Casey Miller and Kate Smith, *Words and Women* (Garden City, NY: Doubleday, 1977).
Wendy Martyna, "Beyond the 'He-Man' Approach: The Case for Non-Sexist Language," *Signs* 5 (1980), 482-93.
Phyllis Trible, *God and the Rhetoric of Sexuality* (Philadelphia: Fortress, 1978).
Inclusive Language in Theology and Worship, Faculty Edition: *Austin Seminary Bulletin* 97/3 (October 1981).
   Five timely essays particularly useful for students in understanding the significance of the language used in describing God and persons' relationships to each other in the light of "God-language."

Backgrounds to Christianity

J. P. V. D. Baldson, *Roman Women: Their History and Habits* (London: Bodley Head, 1962).
   A good review of Roman women's considerable freedom during the period of the Republic.
Phyllis Bird, "Image of Women in the Old Testament" in *Religion and Sexism: Images of Woman in the Jewish and Christian Tradition*, ed. Rosemary Radford Ruether (New York: Simon and Schuster, 1974), pp. 41-88.
   Still one of the standard essays on women's role in the Judaic traditions of Jesus' time.
W. Den Boer, *Private Morality in Greece and Rome: Some Historical Aspects* (Leiden: E. J. Brill, 1979).
   Though the price is prohibitive for students, the book should be on reserve as a must. It serves as a corrective to the generally negative interpretation of women in Greece and Rome.
Keith Hopkins, "Elite Mobility in the Roman Empire," and P. R. C. Weaver, "Social Mobility in the Early Roman Empire: The Evidence of the Imperial Freedmen and Slaves" in *Studies in Ancient Society*, ed. M. I. Finley (London: Routledge & Kegan Paul, 1974), pp. 103-40.
   Both articles deal with the degree of mobility between races and classes and the role of the stratification system in maintaining distinctions.
Sarah B. Pomeroy, *Goddesses, Whores, Wives and Slaves: Women in Classical Antiquity* (New York: Schocken, 1975).

Particularly helpful for comparison of Greek and Roman women's roles and the degree of independence allowed women within their respective societies.

Rosemary Ruether and Eleanor McLaughlin, eds., *Women of Spirit: Female Leadership in the Jewish and Christian Communities* (New York: Simon and Schuster, 1979).
Excellent for discussions of women who played important roles in the social and religious worlds of Judaism and Christianity.

Gail B. Shulman, "Women from the Back of the Synagogue: Women in Judaism" in *Sexist Religion and Women in the Church: No More Silence*, ed. Alice L. Hageman (New York: Association Press, 1974), pp. 143-65.
Good summary of the historical development of Jewish women's roles and the effect of the feminist movement on traditional roles.

Early Christianity

Geoffrey Ashe, *The Virgin* (London: Routledge & Kegan Paul, 1976).
A well-documented, historical study of the cult of Mary; it touches upon many aspects of mythology, theology, and spirituality of women. It is particularly helpful for students working on this as their paper topic. Two other useful texts are Andrew Greeley, *The Mary Myth: On the Feminity of God* (New York: Crossroad, 1977) and Marina Warner, *Alone of All Her Sex: The Myth and the Cult of the Virgin Mary* (New York: Pocket Books, 1976). The latter is more scholarly than Greeley's and gives the student more bibliographical aids.

David L. Balch, *Let Wives be Submissive: The Domestic Code in I Peter*, Monograph Series, 26 (Missoula, MT: Scholars Press, 1981).Critical, exegetical study of I Peter, placing the work within its proper cultural setting. I would recommend it only for the graduate student who has some knowledge of hermeneutical methods.

Kari Elisabeth Børresen, *Subordination and Equivalence: The Nature and Role of Woman in Augustine and Thomas Aquinas* (Washington, DC: University Press of America, 1981).
A critical study of Augustine's and Aquinas' views that women's subordination emerged from the order laid down at creation, while her equality ("equivalence") derived from the order of salvation.

Earl Kent Brown, "Women in Church History: Stereotypes, Archetypes and Operational Modalities," *Methodist History* 18 (January 1980), 109-32.
A study of the way women have throughout Christian history found ways to transcend the stereotypical roles assigned to them by patriarchal views and structures.

Peter Brown, *The Cult of the Saints: Its Rise and Function in Latin Christianity* (Chicago: University of Chicago Press, 1981), pp. 42-49.
These pages give instances of women's roles and participation in the cultic celebrations of departed "saints."

Vern L. Bullough and Bonnie Bullough, *The Subordinate Sex: A History of Attitudes Toward Women* (Baltimore: Penguin Books, 1973).
A study of the various "historical barriers" which have made women's equality the *last* of the inequalities to be overcome.

Carol Christ and Judith Plaskow, eds., *Womanspirit Rising: A Feminist Reader in Religion* (San Francisco: Harper and Row, 1979).
Various essays in this small volume can be used throughout the various sections of the course. The articles present a clear overview of the vital issues raised in contemporary feminist thinking (historical, theological, sociological) and stimulate good discussions.

Elizabeth A. Clark, "Sexual Politics in the Writings of John Chrysostom," *Anglican Theological Review* 59 (1977), 3-20.
A good discussion of female status in fourth century Christianity and an attempt to explain the paradox of Chrysostom's generally negative views on women and his positive, personal friendships with women. Clark raises the same issue in *Jerome, Chrysostom, and Friends: Essays and Translations* (New York: Edwin Mellen Press, 1979), but includes translations of several essays about friendships between men and women in early Christianity.

Mary Daly, *Beyond God the Father: Toward a Philosophy of Women's Liberation* (Boston: Beacon, 1973), and *The Church and the Second Sex* (New York: Harper and Row, 1975 edition).
Both books raise the basic issues of the feminist movement in religion and give the students a handle with which to articulate their views.

Elisabeth Schüssler Fiorenza, *In Memory of Her: A Feminist Theological Reconstruction of Christian Origins* (New York: Crossroad, 1983).
A must for students seriously studying early Christianity. Not only does the author demonstrate how androcentric minds have narrowly selected and falsely interpreted historical data, but she suggests a new feminist hermeneutic to replace the androcentric model.

Roger Gryson, *The Ministry of Women in the Early Church*, trans. Jean Laporte and Mary Louise Hall (Collegeville, MN: Liturgical Press, 1976).
An important study of the deaconess role as it developed and was gradually eliminated in Christian history. It presents canonical sources either justifying or denying leadership to women.

E. Hennecke and W. Schneemelcher, *New Testament Apocrypha* (Philadelphia: Westminster, 1963).
Includes non-canonical sources; e.g., *The Acts of Paul and Thecla*.

Elaine Pagels, *The Gnostic Gospels* (New York: Random House, 1979). Important source for a different perspective on early Christian people and events. Pagels helps the students to reconsider the traditional view of the origins and meanings of Christianity. Equally helpful is Pheme Perkins, *The Gnostic Dialogue: The Early Church and the Crisis of Gnosticism* (New York: Paulist, 1980), particularly pp. 131-41 which deal with women in Gnosticism. A necessary handbook for both sources above is James M. Robinson, ed., *The Nag Hammadi Library* (San Francisco: Harper and Row, 1977).

Rosemary Radford Ruether, *Sexism and God-Talk: Toward a Feminist Theology* (Boston: Beacon Press, 1983). A valuable contribution which carefully examines the basic teachings of the Bible and ancient goddess-oriented cultures. Ruether demonstrates that there are "usable and authentic intimations of divinity within traditional Jewish and Christian understandings of God," and suggests ways of transcending the patriarchal bias in religion.

Letha Scanzoni and Nancy Hardesty, *All We're Meant to Be: A Biblical Approach to Women's Liberation* (Waco, TX: Word Books, 1974). An easily readable summation of the major problems caused by male/female polarity in Christian history, with suggestions for liberation through different approaches and interpretations of the Bible.

Evelyn and Frank Stagg, *Woman in the World of Jesus* (Philadelphia: Westminster, 1978). An analysis of the status of women in Greco-Roman and Judaic cultures, Jesus' attitude towards women, and the New Testament image of women (particularly in Paul, the Synoptics and Acts).

Elisabeth M. Tetlow, *Women and Ministry in the New Testament* (New York: Paulist, 1980). An exploration of the roles and ministries of women in Jesus' time and the early Church, with particular emphasis on biblical foundations of women's status and ministry.

Patricia Wilson-Kastner, et al., *A Lost Tradition: Women Writers of the Early Church* (Washington, DC: University Press of America, 1981). Translations of and introductory essays about four writings of early Christian women (Perpetua, Proba, Egeria, and Eudokia), the earliest extant writings by Christian women.

5

WOMEN IN AMERICAN
CATHOLIC HISTORY

Arlene Swidler

Considering that History and Religious Studies are two of the areas in which feminist scholars have been most active, it is surprising how very little information is compiled in the area of American Catholic Women's History. Catholic Church historians, of course, have never found the laity of great interest, and the contemporary feminist movement has been strongly secular. Protestant and Jewish materials are more easily available, and even those books which purport to address women in American religion in general give only brief attention to Catholicism, often by dealing solely with women in religious orders. So work on American Catholic women remains to be done.

The one exception is books dealing with individual religious orders, partly because of the accessibility of the materials, though I have been gently admonished not to overestimate the order in convent archives. Studies moving wider to focus on sisters in general are still very few, and attempts to integrate these materials with lay women's history have barely begun. People interested in this field will find help in Elizabeth Kolmer, A.S.C., "Catholic Women Religious and Women's History: A Survey of the Literature," *American Quarterly* 30 (1978), 639-51, and in the forthcoming book by Evangeline Thomas, C.S.J., *Women Religious History Sources: A Guide to Archives* (New York: Bowker).

Secular feminist historians, however, have been helpful in raising questions appropriate for Catholic historical research and teaching. For anyone interested in the theory of feminist history I would recommend Gerda Lerner's ninety-two page *Teaching Women's History*, available from the American Historical Association. Professor Lerner, a leader in

Arlene Anderson Swidler teaches in the Department of Religious Studies at Villanova University (Villanova, PA 19085). For the past twenty years she has been active in the Catholic women's movement, publishing articles in that area in such periodicals as the American Benedictine Review, Commonweal, *the* National Catholic Reporter, *and* Spiritual Life. *She served as national chairperson for ecumenical and liturgical affairs for the National Council of Catholic Women from 1966-70 and as editor of NCCW's monthly* Word *in 1970-71. She is the author of* Woman in a Man's Church, *editor of* Sistercelebrations, *co-translator of Haye van der Meer,* Women Priests in the Catholic Church?, *and coeditor of* Women Priests: A Catholic Commentary. *Her most recent book is the edited collection* Human Rights in Religious Traditions *(New York: Pilgrim, 1982).*

this field, is typical of secular feminist historians in showing little interest in religion, and what she says of Catholicism is careless: "Mother Mary Seton was canonized as a saint in 1963." But for a sense of what feminist history is all about and where it is heading, this monograph is superb.

Fortunately, all this de-emphasis on American Catholic women has never been disturbing as I teach my course on American Catholicism. My students have always welcomed the vignettes about women in my lectures, and the knowledge that their own research projects on women will not be cut-and-dried but will require some imagination and initiative is often stimulating for students who see that I too am eager to learn what they come up with.

Beyond the factual material there is always the second focus of the course: Catholic historiography itself, its functions, its trends. Our feminist critique of written history serves as opener to the broader questions. How has the Church community perceived itself? Have we Catholics presumed that ecclesiastical power and jurisdiction were signs of spiritual success? Could, in fact, reading Catholic history encourage an ambitious worldliness? How would we like to see today's events described by a diocesan historian twenty-five years hence, and how do we think they actually will be portrayed? Are Catholic groups more likely than secular groups to attribute accomplishments to whoever was nominally in charge? What are the ethical issues involved in writing church history?

From my teaching of courses on women in religion I have learned that it is necessary to focus on both the positive and the negative effects of organized religion on women, and that the balance must be apparent not simply over the semester but week by week in order to teach a carefully critical approach. The same thing is true of Church history, so that students see not only that women have not always been treated well but also that it was from the Catholic Church that many women drew strength. This bipolar approach can be seen in secular feminist history as well. Although most writers have concentrated on the ways in which women have been oppressed, there has always been a minor stream, of which Mary Beard in her *Woman as Force in History* (New York: Macmillan, 1946) is the best example, which focused on women's activity and accomplishments. By bearing the two sides clearly in mind—seeing strengths and weaknesses simultaneously—students learn the art of loyal criticism.

With these two principles in mind—using the position of women in written history as an opening into discussion of the nature of historiography, and using careful presentation of both positive and negative to encourage thoughtful critical analysis—I find my material falls into three main categories.

Ordinary Women

Like many teachers of both Catholic and secular American history, I include oral reports on family history and ethnicity early in the semester. In my case, teaching near Philadelphia, I like to take up the theme again later by having the students form small teams and visit national parishes to observe liturgies, to interview the pastor, and to hand out questionnaires. In both these assignments I have discovered that the process of putting together questionnaires, whether for guidance in talking with older relatives and neighbors or for congregational distribution, is a stimulating class project. It is also a good opportunity to introduce important ideas about women's roles and lives.

How have ethnic traditions and bonds been maintained? by foods? special celebrations? correspondence with the old country? special celebrations? preserving heirlooms? Who has taken that responsibility? ... How did women immigrants come to this country? with parents? alone? as young wives whose husbands had gone before them? ... Did young families live closer to the husband's or wife's family? With whom did they visit? How often? What was housekeeping like in times past? How were tasks divided? How long did children continue to be born at home, and who assisted? How old were women when they married and had their first child? How many children did they have? Which children were educated? ... When married women worked for money, what kind of jobs did they find? (Some ethnic groups tended toward domestic service, and others toward factory work; still others preferred to take in boarders.) What was life like for women who neither married nor entered the convent? ... How did all these women experience the Church? What did the Church do for them as women? What were they taught was proper behavior for Catholic women?

Extraordinary Women

There is a tendency today to downplay stories of unusual women in favor of social history. I sympathize. To focus on the famous and the unusual is to disparage the women who spend their lives working hard at ordinary jobs, raising families, or teaching other people's children. There is also something sad about women clinging to the image of the lone woman on the periphery of history, rejoicing at the first lady astronaut after all these years.

The situation, however, is somewhat different in Catholic history. Clericalized as we have been, Catholics are still likely to see a kind of sacred aura over many of what are really secular offices within the church. To see a woman fulfilling a role or task commonly filled by priests, then, is not simply to see that a woman can do things or that the system can be flexible; rather, a new understanding of the Church community results. Theological insight is involved. So I find the story of Mary Gwendoline Caldwell as founder of Catholic University, and the strict stipulations she made in offering her money, contributes toward raising consciousness on questions like the accountability of seminaries to the people, who support them and are to be served by their graduates. The stories of Joanna England of the *U.S. Catholic Miscellany* and Katherine Conway of the Boston *Pilot* indicate a recognition of the need for a wide variety of Catholics to be involved in opinion-making.

Another important group of Catholic women worked outside the Church structure. Margaret Brent, the first woman in the colonies to ask for the vote (actually she asked for two, one as a landowner and one as Lord Baltimore's attorney, but got neither), is relevant today. The life of Mother Jones, this country's foremost woman labor organizer, is full of marvelous anecdotes. Dorothy Day is the most current and obvious of these countercultural heroes, all of whom make excellent topics for student oral reports. They too raise methodological questions. Precisely what constitutes "Catholic" history? Are priests in secular roles—like congressman or novelist—more significant for Catholic history than laywomen in those roles?

A third category is "parallel" history, the story of women's work that went on alongside of what is currently presented as Catholic history. Here the stories of women's religious orders are most significant. Current church histories have not integrated the stories of teaching sisters, much less of hospital sisters, into the clerically-oriented history. Oral reports on books about sisters (see Appendix) can fit neatly into the course.

Women as a Class

What has been said and thought about "woman," most often by men, has molded the lives and self-understanding of women. Any discussion of the status of Catholic women today must give some indication of how women reached this position. Certainly something about the attitude of the hierarchical Church toward both the women's suffrage movement and the later Equal Rights Amendment should be included in classroom discussion (see Appendix for suggestions).

One assignment I have used several times involves having the students choose a Catholic periodical to review over a period of years, looking for constants and patterns of change in masthead, contributors (including letters to the editor), style, topics, editorial positions, and even advertising.

This of course can easily be adapted to include women's history. One way is simply to alert all students on such assignments to note the contributions of and attitudes towards women. Another is to let some students focus only on women in some general periodical—

Commonweal, perhaps, or the local diocesan weekly, or, for the more adventurous, Father Coughlin's *Social Justice*. The *N.C.W.C. Review* and its successor, *Catholic Action*, had a good deal of Catholic women's news, especially about local Councils of Catholic Women. Other possibilities are *Hospital Progress* (the official journal of the Catholic Hospital/Health Association), the now defunct *Catholic Nurse*, *Sisters Today*, and *Marriage*. Students reporting on several different periodicals make up an interesting class panel.

Here too questions of Catholic historiography emerge. To what extent and in what ways are we as Church formed by our reading of history and contemporary history? What images of women are fostered by the diocesan press? Are Church-employed women (including but not only sisters) portrayed as being as important as Church-employed men (including but not only priests)? How does ownership affect a periodical? How many magazines are owned by orders of men, and how many by women? Can women and minorities be oppressed not only by the events of history but also by the way that history is recorded?

None of these lectures, discussions or assignments on women has ever been perceived by the class as intrusive. The material on women—and it is, of course, very interesting material—has always been accepted as a proper supplying of what had been lacking. The feminist analysis has been seen as a useful tool to open the whole area of Catholic historiography, its uses and abuses, its implied ecclesiology, its past and its possible future.

Appendix

Articles recommended for assigned reading

A good overall survey of the position of American Catholic women is James J. Kenneally's "Eve, Mary, and the Historians," *Horizons* 3/2 (1976), 187-202. (This article, as well as Kolmer, *supra*, and Oates, *infra*, can also be found in Janet Wilson James, ed., *Women in American Religion* [Philadelphia: University of Pennsylvania Press, 1980].) A good detailed study of women in religious orders is Mary J. Oates's "Organized Voluntarism: The Catholic Sisters in Massachusetts, 1870-1940," *American Quarterly* 30 (1978), 652-80. James J. Kenneally's "Catholicism and Woman Suffrage in Massachusetts," *Catholic Historical Review* 53/1 (1967), 43-57, summarizes clerical opposition over thirty-five years. "Catholics and the E.R.A." by Arlene Swidler, *Commonweal* 103/19 (1976), 585-89, is a historical study focusing primarily on John A. Ryan.

Brief short stories often lead to stimulating discussions. J. F. Powers' "The Lord's Day," a study of the relationship between sisters and their pastor, and "The Valiant Woman," the wry portrait of a pastor and his housekeeper, are both available in *Prince of Darkness* (Garden City, NY: Doubleday, 1947). As an insight into Catholic attitudes toward slavery, Kate Chopin's "La Belle Zoraïde," collected in her *The Awakening and Other Stories* (New York: Holt, Rinehart & Winston, 1970) is useful; though religion is barely mentioned, it is clear that both the slave and her mistress in this tragic love story are Catholics.

Topics suitable for research papers

Women of the past and present worth investigating would include Agnes Repplier, Rose Hawthorne Lathrop, Mary Gordon, Margaret Brent, Mother Cabrini, Elizabeth Seton, Martha Moore Avery and Mother Jones. Students may want to page through *Notable American Women* or *American Women Writers* for other ideas. The writings of various ecclesiastics might be examined: John Lancaster Spalding had surprisingly enlightened views on women. The Maria Monk episode might be worth an oral report; the bibliography in Ewens, *infra*, lists other works of that genre. The Catholic Worker movement, Friendship Houses, women in Catholic higher education, and women in various ethnic groups are possibilities. Ethnic fiction should be rich in insight, yet I have found the quality almost consistently disappointing. Records of local women's groups, schools, parishes, etc. may be available.

Books suitable for reports

Autobiographies are at the top of almost any Women's Studies bibliography. Blandina Segale, S.C., recorded her experiences in the Southwest from 1871 to 1892 in her journal; published as *At the End of the Santa Fe Trail* (Milwaukee: Bruce, 1948), it is widely respected. Dorothy Day's *The Long Loneliness* (New York: Harper, 1952) is often used in courses in women. Madeleva Wolff, C.S.C., outstanding poet and college president, is the author of *My First Seventy Years* (New York: Macmillan, 1959). Somewhat longer but extremely rewarding is Abigail McCarthy's *Private Faces/Public Places* (Garden City, NY: Doubleday, 1972), which recreates a political era. *Rosa, The Life of an Italian Immigrant*, by Marie Hall Ets (Minneapolis: University of Minnesota Press, 1970), qualifies as autobiography; it is the life story of a cleaning woman put together from the stories and reminiscences told to her social-worker friend. Among recent brief autobiographies published by Abingdon are Rosemary Radford Ruether's *Disputed Questions* (1982), heavily theological, and *Hope is an Open Door* (1981) by Mary Luke Tobin, S.L., with recollections of such things as Vatican II and Thomas Merton.

Other possibilities are Mary Ewens' excellent *The Role of the Nun in Nineteenth-Century America* (New York: Arno, 1978) with its helpful bibliography; Ellen Ryan Jolly's *Nuns of the Battlefield* (Providence, RI:

Providence Visitor Press, 1930), an engaging portrait of Civil War sister-nurses; *The New Nuns*, edited by M. Charles Borromeo, C.S.C. (New York: New American Library, 1967), which presents twenty readable articles on changes in religious life; the many biographies of mother founders and histories of various religious orders which can be found in any Catholic library; and such biographies as John N. Kotre's *Simple Gifts: The Lives of Pat and Patty Crowley* (Kansas City, KS: Andrews and McMeel, 1979).

6

FEMINIST THOUGHT AND SYSTEMATIC THEOLOGY
Pauline Turner and Bernard Cooke

Trying to answer the question, "How can a teacher of systematic theology incorporate the insights provided by feminist thinkers?", we faced several major problems and made a few rather arbitrary choices. Ultimately it is impossible to separate systematic theology from biblical or historical studies or distinguish it satisfactorily from the study of spirituality or morality. What we say here, then, must be complemented by the other essays in this series. Besides, the impact of feminist thought on Christian theology is not a peripheral or additional thing; incorporating feminist theology into systematics does not mean only an addition of topics. Rather, the research and reflection of feminist scholars demand revision of our basic approach to doing theology; they recast the basic evidence on which we must reflect; they challenge the presuppositions and methodology with which we previously approached the classic topics of theology.

What we are talking about is not how to teach a special branch or brand of theology, but simply teaching systematic theology more adequately and critically, trying to lead students to understand accurately and personally what is meant by "grace" and "salvation" and "Jesus as the Christ" and "Church" and "God." In our trying to reach this goal, present-day feminist thought has proved a rich and indispensable resource—this we will try to explain in relation to four large areas of what generally is thought of as "systematic theology." Rather than sketch a course in "Systematic Theology from a Feminist Perspective," which would be both interesting and valuable, we will try to indicate ways in which the entire content of theology needs to be changed by feminist understandings.

Theological Anthropology

One of the marks of today's theological enterprise is the emphasis on "the human." It has become a truism that humans—their being and

Pauline Turner did her graduate study in theology at Marquette University. Her most recent teaching position was at Anna Maria College (Paxton, MA 01612). She is presently engaged in research on the role of religion in women's participation in the Nicaraguan revolution.

Bernard Cooke, in the Department of Religious Studies, College of the Holy Cross (Worcester, MA 01610), is immediate past President of the Catholic Theological Society of America. A recipient of the CTSA John Courtney Murray Award, his many writings include Ministry to Word and Sacraments. He is an Associate Editor of Horizons.

consciousness and history—are the basic phenomena that must be studied as a springboard for some insight into the transcendent. This is something quite other than the anthropomorphism by which humans from time immemorial have tended to project their humanness onto their gods. Instead, it is a realization that in trying to understand the ultimate, God, there is nowhere else we can begin except our shared experience of being persons in relation to one another.

As we try to lead students to some notion of a transcendent creator the privileged paradigm is our experienced reality as persons. Even in the context of Christianity as a "revealed religion" where we accept, even though with careful criticism, the belief that there is some communication of the divine to us humans, the only place such revelation could take place is in people's (at least *some* people's) experience. So, in our teaching we initiate discussion and assign reflective or research papers designed to help students understand their own experience as persons, what it means to relate to other persons, what difference relation to the divine might make. Probably in no other place in the teaching of theology do we have such a richness of feminist thought from which to draw in our own classroom lecturing and discussion, in assigning papers, in recommending readings.

Today's reflection by women on what it means to be a woman, in books like Jean Baker Miller, *Towards a New Psychology of Women* (Boston: Beacon, 1976) or Elizabeth Janeway's *Man's World, Woman's Place* (New York: Morrow, 1971) or Penelope Washbourn, *Becoming Woman* (New York: Harper and Row, 1977); feminist recovery of women's side of historical experience, as in Elise Boulding *From the Underside of History* (Boulder, CO: Westview, 1976) or Joyce Erikson, "Women in the Christian Story" (*Cross Currents* 27 [Summer 1977], 183-95); innumerable descriptions in essays and novels and poetry of humanness as experience by the female half of the human race—all this has had major impact on our understanding the very ground out of which we must theologize.

Our goal in courses that deal with theological anthropology is to help our students interpret their experience with realism, historical perspective, and accuracy, to understand in down-to-earth terms what development of Christian personhood involves. We cannot honestly ignore the new feminist insights into what "human" means, the deepened insight we have all gained from Arlene Swidler's *Woman in a Man's Church* (New York: Paulist, 1972) or Margaret Farley's "New Patterns of Relationship" (in Walter J. Burghardt, ed., *Woman: New Dimensions* [New York: Paulist, 1977], pp. 51-70) into the fact that our identity as persons comes not through this or that role—especially not from fulfilling roles culturally designated as appropriately masculine or feminine—but from our being *persons* to one another. Such personal identity is, of course, developed throughout one's life by genuine relationships, relationships which can be enriching only if they respect the fundamental equality of people.

Not surprisingly, the emphasis on personal relationships has triggered an extensive discussion of the appropriate model to guide men/women relations. Rejecting the distortions of male dominance and female subordination, many feminists have been attracted to androgyny as a governing ideal. A second group has opted for the more "conservative" position of a new complementarity between men and women, one that would honor basic equality. Still others have pushed for a unisexist approach; and a fourth position (espoused by Mary Buckley in her address to the 1979 meeting of the Catholic Theological Society of America [*Proceedings* 34: 48-63]) has argued for a transformative person-centered model. In sorting out these positions and working towards a new personal choice, students can be helped by reading Anne Carr, "Theological Anthropology and the Experience of Women" (*Chicago Studies* 19 [1980], 113-28), the CTSA Research Report *Women in Church and Society*, ed. Sara Butler [1978], and Mary Aquin O'Neill, "Towards a Renewed Anthropology" (in *Woman: New Dimensions*, pp. 149-60).

When we teach about the need to move towards a changed understanding of relationships among people, particularly between men and women, our students tend to agree on principle, but what adds passion and realism to that agreement? Our experience is that nothing is more helpful than a historical study of women's oppression, both in the Church and in society. As students read the essays in *Women and Religion*, ed. Elizabeth Clark and Herbert Richardson (New York: Harper and Row, 1977) or the volumes edited by Rosemary Ruether, *Religion and Sexism* (New York: Simon and Schuster, 1974) and *Women of Spirit* (with Eleanor McLaughlin; New York: Simon and Schuster, 1979), they become aware of the continuing story of domination and misogyny that has distorted men/women relations for centuries, and aware of the continuation of such injustice into the present.

There is, of course, the specifically theological aspect of all this, the manner in which each human's transcendent relationship to God is the ultimate foundation for human equality. Here, our teaching in one way or another must take account of the fact that "the true God," the God revealed in Jesus, is an ultimate confirmation of the position taken by feminist theologians. Theism as a distinctive posture towards the divine can be authentic only if it honors a radical equality of humans because they are human. Feminist reflection on this truth, as we find it, for example, in the essays in *Womanspirit Rising*, ed. Carol Christ and Judith Plaskow (San Francisco: Harper and Row, 1979) or in Naomi Goldenberg's *The Changing of the Gods* (Boston: Beacon, 1979) is certainly not pure theory; rather, it is a witness to women's growing awareness that a God who does not respect their full personhood cannot be their God—indeed, cannot be God. Not all students feel comfortable with or accept the feminist critique in such writings, but the challenge to their patriarchal presuppositions can help them discover God as revealed in Jesus of Nazareth.

Several of the most important developments in Christian theology today focus on the notion of "presence," God's presence to humans as the essence of "grace," the guiding power of divine presence as the reality involved in the symbol "divine providence," reassessment of Jesus' presence as risen Lord to the Church. All this builds on contemporary insight into our experience of being present to one another. In trying to convey this to students in a way that educates their personal understandings and not just their "information bank," feminist writings again have proved a great asset.

Explicitly, the stress on personal presence that one finds in essays like Elizabeth Carroll's "Women and Ministry" (in *Woman: New Dimensions*, pp. 84-111) can reinforce and clarify our classroom explanations. But inserting the idea of "presence" into the center of theological discussion involves a basic shift in "models," and here there is an important though implicit feminist contribution.

Presence implies immediacy rather than distance; presence draws attention to human awareness as a *life* process; presence needs to be explained, then, by "organic" rather than "structure" models. Feminist thought has helped us break theologically out of the monopoly held by hierarchical imagery and so has made it possible for us to use "life models" in probing creatively for a theology of presence. Because their painful religious experience has led them to reject the familiar patriarchal images of "hierarchy" and to search for some other approach to the God of Christianity, feminist theologians—including those who feel they can no longer fit within the Christian theological tradition— provide glimpses of the theology that can emerge from reflecting on our presence to one another as human persons.

Before leaving discussion of theological anthropology some mention should be made, though it is not our topic, of the important work being done on Christian women's spirituality by theologians such as Sandra Schneiders and Joann Wolski Conn.

Christology

Whatever distinctiveness Christian theological anthropology possesses comes in terms of christology, which for about four decades has been undergoing major development. Communicating some insight into this more recent theology of Jesus as the Christ is critical at a time when, because of our cultural exposure to other great world religions, our students (as well as as ourselves) must face the question of the distinctiveness and universality of Jesus as savior.

One feature of this "new" christology is a keener appreciation of the genuine humanness of Jesus of Nazareth. Biblical and historical studies have helped us to reconstruct much of the Jewish world in which Jesus lived and to situate him in that space-time context. By examining Jesus' dealings with women as part of that effort, feminist theologians, particularly New Testament scholars like Elisabeth Schüssler Fiorenza (whose recent *In Memory of Her* [New York: Crossroad, 1983] is a must for anyone studying Jesus and the emergence of Christianity) have provided the kind of understanding that helps students realize that Jesus was actually an ordinary human and yet different in a profoundly revolutionary way.

More aware of how truly "scandalous" and revolutionary Jesus' dealings with women were, we have been led to discover the radical social reorientation implied in his teaching and public ministry. It is not just that Jesus was kind and considerate of women; what is involved is an underlying rejection of the chauvinism intrinsic to the patriarchal culture of his day. In communicating to our students this aspect of Jesus' public career we are providing them with an understanding that is essential to their acquiring a genuinely Christian world view.

However, we have found that dealing with Jesus' attitude towards women and searching for its grounding has led us to a deepened insight into what was the key to Jesus' preaching and healing ministry, his experience of God as his "Abba." As with the Israelitic prophets before him, Jesus' discontent with the cultural and religious situation of his day flowed from his unique awareness of the divine. The God he experienced as "Abba" was incompatible with anything but a complete equality of all persons, regardless of social or sexual discrimination.

Such reflection reveals Jesus' radical challenge to the social structures of patriarchalism and to the social injustices intrinsic to those structures. Though, as Phyllis Trible indicates in "Depatriarchalizing in Biblical Interpretation" (*Journal of the American Academy of Religion* 41 [1973], 30-48), the deepest currents of Israelitic thought already contain an element of depatriarchalizing, what God did (and does) in Jesus is a revolutionary liberation of the human social and cultural order. The God revealed in Jesus demands a much different world than the one in which we live, in which the marginalization of people denies them the dignity that Jesus respected in all those he encountered.

One of the most recent and still inchoative shifts in christology is towards *Christ*-ology, i.e., towards a study of Jesus becoming "the Christ" with his resurrection. The historical career of Jesus is intrinsic to this redemptive role and indeed provides the only concrete source for understanding who and what Jesus is. Yet, the New Testament writings clearly state that it is with his passage through death into new life that Jesus gains full possession of the Spirit and full saving power to transform human history. Christian soteriology cannot be restricted, then, to reflection about the person and activity of the historic Jesus; it must deal primarily with the saving action that began with Calvary and Easter and that continues until the eschaton, i.e., with Jesus' action as the Christ.

However, that "Christ-phase" of Jesus' saving ministry is carried on through his embodiment in the Christian community, the mystery that Paul describes as "body of Christ" and the Johannine tradition as "the vine and the branches." Here we find a challenging convergence with feminist questioning about the appropriateness of a male savior for women. The fact that the risen one is embodied in and finds saving expression through a community made up of both women and men means that "the savior" of humans is not just this one isolated historical male, Jesus of Nazareth. Christians, women and men, need not turn to a *male* savior with all the patriarchal implications this would have. Challenged by several feminist thinkers to confront this issue, which is clearly basic to any Christian woman's spirituality—as a matter of fact to the spirituality of any Christian, we have been led to grapple creatively with the role played by the Christian community in the ongoing process of salvation. In our teaching we have found that discussion and papers dealing with "the Christian community as co-savior with Christ" have helped many students to gain a more realistic understanding of what is involved in Jesus' redemptive activity and so be prepared to appreciate better the changed role of Catholics in a post-Vatican II Church.

Ecclesiology

Inevitably the topic of christology has led us into ecclesiology, an area that is becoming difficult to define. Even though it is inseparable from christology as we have just described it and inseparable from a broadened approach to sacramental theology, theological focus on the Church does provide us a context for discussing three intersections with today's feminist thought. The first and probably most evident one has to do with ministry, the second deals with equality in the Church, the third with our models for thinking about the Church.

The last-named, our models for the Church, is probably the most basic. After books like Avery Dulles, *Models of the Church* (Garden City, NY: Doubleday, 1978) it is "old hat" to talk about some shift away from the patriarchal model for thinking about the Christian community. But shift *from* implies shift *to*; what model is more appropriate than a political or patriarchal one? The question is complicated by the fact that we have employed the patriarchal model not only for the Church but for all reality. By suggesting consensus or friendship or life-support patterns for community, feminist writing such as Sandra Schneiders'

"Women in the Fourth Gospel and the Role of Women in the Contemporary Church" (*Biblical Theology Bulletin* 12 [1982], 35-45) has provided alternative models for our ecclesiology.

The change from a hierarchical world view is so drastic and far-reaching that it requires constant sensitizing to the patriarchal assumptions that color our outlook on practically every aspect of human experience. Feminist writings on sexist language, on the impact of exclusively male symbolizing in our liturgical ceremonies, on sexist role modelling in society are all materials upon which our teaching can draw in order to open students' minds and imaginations to understanding the Church as essentially a community of persons, "the people of God," who share faith and hope and a ministry of service.

It is intrinsic to "hierarchy" that it suggest inequality among the members of the Church; there are some who are "higher" and some who are "lower"; the Church as a community is stratified. History indicates unmistakably how quickly such division arose and how persistently it has characterized the Church's life. Feminist historians and biblical scholars—the essays in *Women and Priesthood*, ed. Carroll Stuhlmueller (Collegeville, MN: Liturgical Press, 1980) are a good example—have made solid contributions to correcting this view, showing that Christianity in its very early decades was marked by a revolutionary acceptance of women as equal members of the Body of Christ. Reconstructing the life of primitive Christianity is not just a matter of rehabilitating women as Christians; to the extent that our teaching can convey this historical reality we can recapture some understanding of what it means to say that the Church is a community of believers, bonded as brothers and sisters by faith in Jesus as the Christ.

Equality is not a matter of privilege; it is a right with correlative responsibilities, which implies that Christians should bear responsibility for the mission and ministry of the church, no matter what their particular situation in society or in the Christian community. Such a ministry should be commensurate with people's distinctive talents and opportunities; it should not be grounded on the status presumptions of a patriarchal structure. Yet, until the recent move of women towards equal participation in the life of the Church, epitomized by but in no way limited to "women's ordination," most of us were scarcely alerted to the inequity of denying full ministerial opportunity to women because of their sex. Even now, many college students react with less than enthusiasm to the notion of full sharing by women in the ministry of the church.

In working to counteract this prejudice we can draw from a large body of feminist writing, much of it triggered by the 1976 papal *Declaration on the Admission of Women to the Ministerial Priesthood*. Two of the most extensive reactions to that document were *Women Priests* (New

York: Paulist, 1976) edited by Arlene and Leonard Swidler and the Concilium volume *Women in the Church* (New York: Seabury, 1980) edited by Virgil Elizondo and Norbert Greinacher. At the same time, New Testament research into the origins of Christian ministry has revealed the open acceptance of women's ministry in the earliest decades of the Church. To have students discover this, through reading books like Elisabeth Schüssler Fiorenza, *In Memory of Her* or Elizabeth Tetlow, *Women and Ministry in the New Testament* (New York: Paulist, 1980), can help them realize that there is nothing God-given about the present exclusion of women from full ministry and that full involvement of women is intrinsic to the life of the Church.

Feminist theology dealing with questions of Church order and ministry provides some of the most insightful and educationally provocative material for teaching the "new" view of the Church that has come with Vatican II. Though women's role in the Church has tended to be their focus, women theologians have increasingly broadened their discussion to criticize long-standing clerical monopoly of ministry and to stress Vatican II's enfranchisement of the laity.

God-Talk

Our ultimate challenge as teachers of theology comes when we try to lead students to a relatively non-idolatrous understanding of God. Here the challenge and contribution of feminist thought have been most profound. Much contemporary philosophy of religion has focused on "God-talk"; feminist discussion of sexist language has naturally and critically intersected with this and with foundational theology. The decade between Mary Daly's *Beyond God the Father* (Boston: Beacon, 1973) and Rosemary Ruether's recent *Sexism and God-Talk* (Boston: Beacon, 1983) has witnessed a growing awareness of the extent to which patriarchal outlooks have been enshrined in religious and theological language about the transcendent.

Feminist literature tends, and rightly so, to emphasize the affront to women's religious sensitivities in such patriarchal assumptions. The theological issue involved is idolatry. If we are to teach Christianity as a monotheistic religion, as a faith and not an ideology, we must work to purify God-talk and God-thought and God-imagery from the limitations imposed by constant reference to God as male in our present religious language. Use of male metaphor with almost total neglect of balancing female metaphor has led to a distortion of understanding that impacts negatively on the religious experience of both women and men, but specially on women's sense of self-worth and identity. In trying to remedy this imbalance, our teaching experience suggests that the most important element may be our own sensitive use of language in the classroom, so that non-sexist ways of referring to God help communicate a non-patriarchal understanding of the divine. Style sheets on non-sexist use of language, for example, that issued by the *Journal of Ecumenical Studies* to its authors, provide practical ways of dealing with this language problem.

During the two millenia of Christian effort to probe the mystery of God one of the favorite scripture passages from which theologians have worked is Genesis 1:27. With its reference to humans being created "in the image of God" the passage suggests that human persons somehow mirror and therefore lead to an understanding of the divine but suggests also that humanity should be seen in relationship to the divine. For centuries the passage was a favorite one for reflecting on the nature of "the human" but also a favorite for justifying, through faulty exegesis, the superiority of men over women. Tracing the exegetical history of this passage provides an excellent way of tracing the denigration of women that has marked most of Christian history; but it also provides us with the opportunity to show how this denial of equal humanity to women distorted Christianity's understanding of both "the human" and "the divine." Criticizing the faulty exegesis of Genesis 1:27 provides a natural opening to explain how the dialectic of human personal relations, especially those between men and women can function sacramentally as a revelation of God.

Working out the implications of a non-sexist interpretation of "image of God" is only part of a broader pedagogical challenge: to explain how human experience can function as springboard for theological reflection. One of the key breakthroughs in contemporary theology has been the realization that our experience, individual and corporate, is the only ultimate "word" that speaks existentially to us about the reality of the divine. If our students are to know this personally as a realization of their own, they must learn to discern the "traces of the divine" in their own experience; but this can occur only to the extent that their experience is authentically person, open, and unprejudiced.

Actually, much of our dealing with one another is distorted by prejudice, prejudice that is embodied in societal structures that marginate and oppress people, prejudice of which we often are not even aware. Feminist challenge to the prejudiced dealings between men and women has become a powerful force in creating a more open, balanced understanding of the manner in which humans, and Christians in particular, should deal with one another. Feminist attacks on sexism have highlighted the extent to which human relationships are touched by sin and in need of redemption. As one of the most outspoken voices in the movement of "liberation theology," feminist theology has categorized sexism as "social sin" that is intertwined with other forms of oppression and discrimination. To emphasize that this judgment upon sexism is solidly grounded in basic Catholic teaching, it helps to refer students to the 1981 pastoral letter, *Male and Female God Created Them*, of Bishops Victor Balke and Raymond Lucker.

While women theologians like Letty Russell in *Human Liberation in a Feminist Perspective* (Philadelphia: Westminster, 1974) and *Growth in Partnership* (Philadelphia: Westminster, 1981) and Madonna Kolbenschlag in *Kiss Sleeping Beauty Good-Bye* (New York: Bantam, 1981) point to the injustices and oppression, the marginalization and prejudice that have marked relations between the sexes and resulted in the wounding and diminution of women as persons, they also point to the way to liberation from these evils. As June O'Connor details in "Liberation Theologies and the Women's Movement: Points of Comparison and Contrast" (*Horizons* 2 [1975], 103-15), feminist soteriology agrees substantially with other liberation theologies, especially in its emphasis on "self help."

Combining the notion of *praxis*, i.e., that genuine reflection upon human society demands involvement in the effort to overcome social injustice, with Vatican II's teaching that "establishing the kingdom of God" means working to better the human condition, feminist theologians have stressed the many-faceted character of liberation. The servitudes imposed by unjust social structures are apparent, the oppressions coming from prejudiced attitudes less evident. More hidden is "the enemy within," the interiorizing by women (as well as by other marginated groups) of the ideology and values that legitimate the oppressive social situation. Only the oppressed can free themselves from this inner enslavement, hence the importance of "conscienticization," awakening persons to a more genuine understanding of themselves, of the forces that shape their lives, and of the possibilities of fashioning their own destiny. Knowing that such a change in perspective cannot occur apart from changes in social institutions, feminist theologians have been a catalytic force in women's struggle for equality, especially equality in the Church.

Explaining all this to students places soteriology in a new down-to-earth context; it creates a different, more realistic, understanding of "salvation" or "redemption" or "divine providence." It can lead to awareness of the role that human endeavor is meant to play in the work of salvation, to awareness that salvation must touch human society as well as individuals, and to awareness of the systemic nature of much of the evil in the world. Ultimately, a religion's ability to justify its god rests in its ability to take account of the evil that humans experience. Feminist theology has not proposed a solution to the problem of evil; it has contributed importantly to our thinking more realistically and hopefully about it, and so contributed to our understanding of the God revealed in Jesus, the Christ.

Additional Bibliography

Helpful on feminist theological methodology are L. Iglitzin and R. Ross, eds., *Women in the World* (Santa Barbara, CA: Clio, 1976); Phyllis Trible, *God and the Rhetoric of Sexuality* (Philadelphia: Fortress, 1978); and Elisabeth Schüssler Fiorenza, "You are not to be called Father," *Cross Currents* 29 (1979), 301-22. A valuable bibliographical tool is Anne Patrick, "Women and Religion: A Survey of Significant Literature, 1965-1974" in *Woman: New Dimensions*, pp. 161-89; also valuable are the bibliographies and symposia published in *Listening* (1978-1980). Helpful topical studies are: Letty Russell, *The Future of Partnership* (Philadelphia: Westminster, 1979); Elizabeth Janeway, *The Powers of the Weak* (New York: Quill, 1981); Rosemary Ruether and Rosemary Keller, eds., *Women and Religion in America* (San Francisco: Harper & Row, 1981); Rosemary Ruether, "Where Are They Heading?" *Christianity and Crisis*, April 4, 1983, pp. 111-16; Diane Tennis, "Reflections on the Maleness of Jesus," *Cross Currents* 28 (1978), 137-41; and Herman Mertens, "Feminist Theology," *Theology Digest* 30 (1982), 103-106.

7

FEMINIST ETHICS IN THE CHRISTIAN ETHICS CURRICULUM

Margaret A. Farley

The incorporation of feminist issues and feminist methods and sources into a Christian ethics curriculum is at once a simple and a complex enterprise. It is simple because a feminist approach to ethics can be made explicit at almost every juncture in the curriculum. It is complex because feminist ethics is, like most other general approaches to ethics, pluralistic. Moreover, as a systematic discipline it is in its beginning stages, and there are few comprehensive sources to which students can turn for analytical foundations. The difficulties which students and teachers face in building a syllabus for feminist ethics, however, are not essentially different from those we confront in much of the teaching of ethics. That is, controversy demands the use of a variety of sources; most of the appropriate readings are to be found in short essays rather than in book-length treatments; and since ethics is in many respects a derivative discipline, significant materials must be drawn from many other areas of learning, including theology, biblical studies, and the behavioral, social, and natural sciences.

I shall try in this essay to reflect both the simplicity and complexity of "mainstreaming" feminist ethics into a general curriculum of Christian ethics, or moral theology. Beginning with some general comments regarding feminist ethics, I want then to focus on specific places where feminist contributions can be introduced into a variety of courses. Here I will distinguish what might be called foundational issues in ethics (both methodological and substantive) from what we often call "problems" or "topics" in special ethics. My concern will be with what many consider "personal" rather than "social" issues in ethics (since the latter will be emphasized in another essay in this series). It will, however, be readily apparent that these categories are difficult to keep separate. This is true generally for much of contemporary ethics, but it is especially true for feminists who have long argued that "the personal is political."

Margart A. Farley teaches Christian Ethics in the Divinity School, Yale University (New Haven, CT 06510). In addition to A Metaphysics of Being and God, *her many writings include "New Patterns of Relationship: Beginnings of a Moral Revolution" (Theological Studies, 1975), "Sources of Sexual Inequality in the History of Christian Thought" (Journal of Religion, 1976), and "Beyond the Formal Principles" (Journal of Religious Ethics, 1979). Her essay "The Church and the Family: An Ethical Task" appeared in Horizons 10/1 (Spring 1983). She has served on the CTSA Board of Directors.*

Feminist Ethics

One way to identify a common core for feminist ethics is to look at presently available key texts. Though there is not yet one volume that claims to offer a comprehensive feminist ethical theory, there are several which provide a good overview of the commitments, methods, and common issues that characterize feminist ethics today. Beverly Wildung Harrison's *Our Right to Choose: Toward a New Ethic of Abortion* (Boston: Beacon, 1983) is a straightforward ethical work, though it is limited by intention to ethical analysis relevant to the issue of abortion. Despite its social focus, however, this book offers elements for a general theological ethic. There are several volumes which provide constructive work in feminist theology and biblical studies, and which include both analyses and recommendations with clear relevance for Christian ethics. Among these are Rosemary Radford Ruether's *Sexism and God-Talk: Toward a Feminist Theology* (Boston: Beacon, 1983); Letty M. Russell's *The Future of Partnership* (Philadelphia: Westminster, 1979); and Elisabeth Schüssler Fiorenza's *In Memory of Her: A Feminist Theological Reconstruction of Christian Origins* (New York: Crossroad, 1983). There are also a growing number of anthologies and collections of essays which make available a variety of historical, philosophical, psychological, and sociological studies that are essential to the doing of feminist theological ethics. I include among these: Rosemary Radford Ruether, ed., *Religion and Sexism* (New York: Simon & Schuster, 1974); Sheila Greeve Davaney, ed., *Feminism and Process Thought* (New York: Mellen, 1981); Rosemary Agonito, ed., *History of Ideas on Women* (New York: Paragon, 1977); Mary Vetterling-Braggin, *et al.*, eds., *Feminism and Philosophy* (Totowa, NJ: Littlefield, Adams, 1978); Carol Gould, ed., *Beyond Domination: New Perspectives on Women and Philosophy* (Totowa, NJ: Littlefield, Adams, 1983); Jo Freeman, ed., *Women: A Feminist Perspective* (Palo Alto, CA: Mayfield, 1979); Michelle Zimbalist Rosaldo and Louise Lamphere, eds., *Woman, Culture, and Society* (Stanford, CA: Stanford University Press, 1974); Jean Strouse, ed., *Women and Analysis* (New York: Dell, 1974). With these few texts in hand, one can discern both the pluralism that marks feminist ethics and the shared values and issues which identify it as feminist. Out of these texts, too, can come the questions which constitute the major entry-points for feminist ethics into traditional courses in Christian ethics.

The pluralism in feminist ethics, of course, mirrors the pluralism in feminism in general. It is largely traceable to different analyses of the causes of sexism and different strategies for overcoming it. The works I have just cited do not so much represent this pluralism as provide second-level reflection on it and some correspondingly helpful typologies. Thus, for example, a "liberal" feminist ethic can be identified that critiques failures to extend the liberal tradition of political rights to women, and that advocates "reform" of discriminatory policies of gender role-differentiation. "Socialist" feminist ethics are identified as primarily concerned with the need to change economic structures in society in order to secure true equality and autonomy for women. A "radical" feminist ethic is located in the belief that the only way to alleviate women's oppression is to achieve complete political, economic, sexual, and reproductive freedom for women, even at the price of separatism or the reversal of assignments of power according to gender. Typologies which are more or less variations on these themes, and which apply to both the private and the public spheres of life, can be found in Alison Jaggar's essay, "Political Philosophies of Women's Liberation" (*Feminism and Philosophy*, pp. 5-21); in Ruether, *Sexism and God-Talk*, chapters 1, 4, and 9; and in an essay by Carol Robb, "A Framework for Feminist Ethics," *The Journal of Religious Ethics* 9/1 (Spring 1981), 48-68.

The pluralism in feminism and feminist ethics, however, does not obscure an essential common core of issues and even basic principles. A firm methodological commitment is maintained to a focus on the experience of women as the primary source for feminist ethics. The most fundamental substantive principle which feminist ethicists share might be formulated in terms such as these: Women are fully human and are to be valued as such. Feminist ethics in its most general sense refers, after all, to any ethical theory which locates its roots in feminism, and especially in the contemporary feminist movement. Feminism, in its most fundamental meaning, is a conviction and a movement opposed to discrimination on the basis of gender. Since gender discrimination (sexism) has been largely discrimination against women, feminism aims to correct this bias by a bias for women. This includes a strategically primary concern for the well-being of women and a taking account of women's experience as a way to understand what well-being means for women and men.

To identify feminist ethics with these bare assertions, however, could risk trivializing its central insights. In order to understand the significance of a feminist approach to Christian theological ethics, then, it is necessary to specify further the principle of nondiscrimination and to investigate shared feminist commitments to certain values and to the transformation of patterns of interpersonal and social relationships. Major questions in feminist philosophy and theology that have entailed ethical issues for feminists (and that are treated at length in the volumes cited above) include: the nature of the human self (including the meaning of embodiment, the place of freedom within the human personality, and the possibilities for moral development); integrity and fairness in patterns and structures of relationship (both personal and political); the value of the world of nature. It is these questions, too, that are frequently part of the agenda of traditional courses in Christian ethics, and it is in relation to them that feminist analysis can be used both to sharpen and transform key historical and contemporary ethical issues.

Joining the Issues

No matter how traditional a curriculum in Christian ethics, or moral theology, may be, it is probably the case that feminist issues are relevant to every course. Feminist theologians came to the conclusion long ago that the whole of Christian theology must be rethought in profound ways if we are to take seriously a commitment to feminism and to Christian faith. Once we are aware of the importance of the feminist critique of every major doctrine of the Christian churches (whether the doctrine of God, the doctrine of creation, redemptive incarnation, and the church, or the doctrine of the human person, eschatology, or any other important doctrine), then we are aware, too, of the need for revision and reconstruction. Faith itself is injured unless these tasks are undertaken, and the practice of faith in the life of the church and society is diminished unless the consequences of such tasks are taken seriously. So, then, it is not surprising that theological ethics, as well as theology, is in every respect a candidate for feminist critique, reconstruction, and renewal. This is not only because it is subject to a feminist "hermeneutic of suspicion," but because major concerns, deep within our contemporary struggles in theological ethics, can be illuminated by the new questions which feminists raise. My primary intention in what follows is not to delineate possible feminist positions, but to show some of the places in Christian ethics where these questions are appropriate and beneficial.

Questions of Method

There are three fairly obvious methodological issues for which feminist analysis is especially relevant. The first of these has to do with current debate regarding the meaning and validity of deontological and teleological patterns of ethical reasoning. Feminist ethics offers, at the very least, particularly acute "cases in point" for students' examination of the adequacy of these modes of reasoning and ethical justification. Feminist ethics thus far tends to insist explicitly on the importance of both types of reasoning (Harrison, chap. 1). There is a concern to establish, on the one hand, a basis for judging certain human actions unethical precisely because these actions contradict fundamental understandings of what it means to be a human person. On the other hand, feminists are concerned with the consequences of human action, and for an ethical assessment of means in relation to ends and parts in relation to wholes. To say these things does not mean that feminist ethics settles *a priori* all the controverted issues regarding what does or does not constitute an

inviolable feature of human nature, or what constellation of values de-
termines all relativizing decisions. It does mean that feminist questions
regarding respect for persons, an integrated view of the human self, new
patterns of human relationships, and an ecological view of persons and
things within a shared universe, almost inevitably demand the opening
of ethical inquiry to a consideration of all the possible ways of resolving
conflicts, and an opening of ethical analysis to considerations of rights
as well as needs, goals as well as duties, contexts as well as principles.

A second methodological issue for which feminist ethics provides
an intriguing set of questions relates more to ethical epistemology than
to logic. It should be of great interest to students of Christian ethics that
much of feminist ethics incorporates a realistic epistemology and is
amenable to some interpretations of natural law theory. Of course,
feminist ethics is not univocal in this regard, and in fact it almost always
includes a highly specific critique of certain visions of natural law (those
versions whose method or content allow the perpetuation of false interpretations of women's reality and the continuation of structures
which feminists deem to be injurious to individuals and groups). This
very critique, however, affirms the requirement that ethics attend to the
concrete reality of persons, however inevitably partial the insight and
provisional the interpretation. Feminist ethics has its origin, like the
origin of feminism generally, in women's growing awareness that our
own reality as women-persons was falsely understood by religious and
philosophical traditions. The dissonance between women's own developing self-understanding and that imposed upon us from without
suggests both the difficulties and the possibilities of access to reality as
intelligible, to reality attainable in some degree by reflection on lived
experience. Feminist ethics does not deny the historical nature of
knowledge, nor the influence of the human context upon its development. Yet it presupposes some means of discerning mistaken views of
reality, and some criteria whereby interpretations can be judged more or
less accurate and adequate.

Finally, and closely related to what I have just noted, feminist
ethics, like feminist theology, raises important questions and provides
significant vantage points for understanding current debates about hermeneutical theory. Feminist scholars generally are struggling with the
formulation of feminist hermeneutical principles which will function in
the interpretation of all the sources for feminist theology and ethics—
whether the Bible, the history of theology, related disciplines, or contemporary experience (Fiorenza, chap. 1; Ruether, *Sexism and God-
Talk*, chap. 2). Decisions about the use and construal of sources for
Christian ethics is an ongoing concern for the discipline as a whole.
Feminist ethics provides particularly apt illustrations of the problems of
bringing together the horizons of a tradition and the horizons of present

experience. It exhibits the possibilities of different hermeneutical approaches whether one is asking the meaning of an historical text, the ethical implications of economic structures, or the kind of responsibility assumed for the preservation of the human species.

Thematic and Substantive Questions

I shall point to only two of the many possible large issues which courses in Christian ethics can be expected to address, and for which feminist Christian ethics offers important questions. The first of these is the many-sided issue of the *nature of the human self*. Ethical principles and action-guides, as well as theories of virtue or character, depend to a great extent on our identification of features of human personhood, our interpretation of the integral relationship of these features, and our understanding of human limitations and possibilities. Feminist ethics raises critical questions regarding traditional theories in all of these regards.

Feminist ethics has, for example, a special concern to explore the meaning of autonomy as the feature of personhood that grounds a requirement of respect for persons. Some years ago, feminists brought women's experience to bear in a Nietzschean-like critique of Christian self-understanding. (Mary Daly's earlier works, *Beyond God the Father* [Boston: Beacon, 1973], and *Gyn/Ecology* [Boston: Beacon, 1978], as well as *Pure Lust* [Boston: Beacon, 1984], are especially relevant here.) That is, they pressed the question of whether or not Christianity is finally a religion for the weak and dependent, a religion for victims, a religion that reinforces passivity and makes a virtue out of the self-sacrifice of the resentful. Those aspects of Christian teaching that have been used in this way to promote a certain self-understanding for women had to be critiqued. Hence, feminists took seriously the human characteristics of freedom and autonomy, claiming them for women as well as for men. At the same time, feminist ethics became critical of the post-Enlightenment emphasis on these characteristics, and the individualism to which it led (Whitbeck, in Gould; Saiving, in Davaney). Feminist contributions, then, to the present debate regarding the status of "relationality" as a feature of personhood (along with freedom and autonomy) have further pressed the need for more adequate views of the human self. This need is reinforced by new studies in moral development (e.g., Carol Gilligan, *In A Different Voice* [Cambridge: Harvard University Press, 1982]), as well as by the growing concern in Christian ethics generally for clarification of our understanding of the "social self," of human "solidarity," of a human nature that has at its heart both freedom and a capacity (and need) for relation.

A second major issue in Christian ethics which can be illuminated by the questions of feminist ethics follows closely upon the first. It is the issue of *patterns and norms, models and structures, for human relationships*. Just as feminist analysis insists on holding together autonomy and relationality in a view of the human self, so it struggles to hold together principles of equality and mutuality as fundamental norms (or at least goals) for human relationships. Once again, debates which in Christian ethics may take the form of liberalism versus romanticism are entered by feminists in ways that critique the inadequacies of both (Ruether; Whitbeck, in Gould). Feminists seldom claim to have the ultimate design for family, church, or society, but they do attempt to demonstrate the need for justice in the form of basic human equality and a principle of mutuality. Holding the two together, despite the complex and difficult questions thereby entailed, yields a preferred model for relationship at all levels which is characterized by collaboration rather than by domination and subjugation or by opposition and competition (Russell).

Beginning with a critique of sexism in private and public relations, feminist ethics argues for corresponding critiques of social, economic, or political arrangements that fail to respect the freedom, dignity, and basic needs for well-being of every person. Hence, feminist ethics includes a critique of racism and classism, and of imperialism and religious intolerance (Ruether). The questions it raises are questions of participation in political power and fair distribution of economic resources. Often closely aligned with liberation theology, sometimes with liberal or radical socialism, and other theories and movements whose social analysis yields strong criticism of the status quo, feminist ethics universalizes its principles from the perceived logical and moral demand to extend insights gained first from the experience of the disadvantaged position of women. Feminist ethics is a social ethics (Robb), and that is because it recognizes that there are always structures in the public realm that make possible the continuation of just or unjust structures in the private.

Additional bibliographical resources for incorporating feminist ethics into general courses in Christian ethics include: Simone de Beauvoir, *The Second Sex* (New York: Vintage, 1974); Walter Burghardt, ed., *Woman: New Dimensions* (New York: Paulist, 1975); Carol Christ and Judith Plaskow, eds., *Womanspirit Rising* (San Francisco: Harper, 1979); Jean Bethke Elshtain, *Public Man, Private Woman: Women in Social and Political Thought* (Princeton, NJ: Princeton University Press, 1981); Dexter Fisher, ed., *The Third Woman: Minority Women Writers of the United States* (Boston: Houghton Mifflin, 1980); Alison Jaggar, *Feminist Politics and Human Nature* (Totowa, NJ: Rowman & Allenheld, 1983); Nannerl Keohane, *et al.*, *Feminist Theory: A Critique of Ideology* (Chicago: University of Chicago Press, 1982); Juliet Mitchell, *Woman's Estate* (New York: Vintage, 1973); Cherrie Moraga and Gloria Anzaldua, eds., *This Bridge Called My Back: Writings by Radical Women of Color* (Watertown, MA: Persephone Press, 1981); Rosalind Rosenberg, *Beyond*

Separate Spheres: Intellectual Roots of Modern Feminism (New Haven, CT: Yale University Press, 1982); Letty Russell, *Becoming Human* (Philadelphia: Westminster, 1982); *Women in Dialogue: Inter-American Meeting, Puebla, Mexico* (Notre Dame, IN: Catholic Committee on Urban Ministry, 1979). Types of literature other than historical/analytical that can be helpful include: novels, such as Margaret Atwood's *Bodily Harm* (New York: Bantam, 1983); Marge Piercy's *Small Changes* (New York: Fawcett, 1972); Alice Walker's *The Color Purple* (New York: Harcourt Brace Jovanovich, 1982); reflections, such as Susan Griffin's *Woman and Nature* (New York: Harper, 1978); Robin Morgan's *The Anatomy of Freedom* (Garden City, NY: Doubleday Anchor, 1982); Adrienne Rich's *On Lies, Secrets, and Silence* (New York: Norton, 1979); sociological-biographical studies, such as Robert Coles and Jane Hallowell Coles, *Women of Crisis*, 2 vols. (New York: Delacorte, 1978, 1980); poetry, such as Joanna Bankier, et al., eds., *The Other Voice: Twentieth Century Women's Poetry in Translation* (New York: Norton, 1976); Laura Chester and Sharon Barba, eds., *Rising Tides: Twentieth Century Women Poets* (New York: Washington Square Press, 1973); Adrienne Rich, *The Dream of a Common Language* (New York: Norton, 1978); Penelope Washbourn, *Seasons of Woman: Song, Poetry, Ritual, Prayer, Myth, Story* (San Francisco: Harper, 1979).

Issues in Special and Applied Ethics

Given the nature of feminist ethical concerns for the large issues in theological anthropology, political philosophy, and moral development, it is not surprising that feminist ethics appears frequently in specialized courses where these concerns more directly touch lived experience. The questions of feminist ethics are more obvious, if not more urgent, here. Since the available literature for these courses is massive, and there are many ways in which feminist approaches may be introduced, I will only sketch some possibilities for courses or course segments in two somewhat general areas: sexual ethics and medical ethics. Similar sketches could be made for areas such as ethics and spirituality, ethics and economics (including, especially, questions of work, production, poverty), the ethics of power, and ethics and the environment.

Sexual Ethics

Over the years I have frequently co-taught a course in sexual ethics. The design of the course represents convictions that (a) norms for sexual behavior cannot be discerned without a broad-based view of the meaning of human sexuality; (b) the development of an adequate contemporary Christian sexual ethic requires an examination, interpretation, and assessment of the traditional sources for such an ethic; (c) Christian sexual ethics today is importantly pluralistic, so that if students are to discern norms in an informed and disciplined way, it is helpful for them to examine more than one view on key controversial issues. Given these convictions, and given my delineation of major methodological and substantive concerns in feminist ethics (above), it may be evident how a feminist approach is generally relevant. I can, however, make this more explicit simply by indicating topics explored in class sessions and some of the more explicitly feminist readings which provide background for these sessions.

The course has been structured to include sessions on (1) the human person as embodied and sexual; (2) biblical perspectives on human sexuality; (3) historical theological perspectives (both Roman Catholic and Protestant); (4) social-scientific perspectives; (5) the significance of gender; (6) the negative and positive power of sex; (7) sexuality, love, and commitment; (8) marriage and family; (9) male homosexuality and lesbianism; (10) critical normative reconstruction: developing an adequate contemporary Christian sexual ethic. Some of these topics take more than one session. At each point along the way feminist interpretive questions can be introduced, in regard to historical as well as contemporary materials.

Let me first indicate some bibliographical resources which, though they are not identified as overtly feminist, nonetheless are extremely helpful for the framing of feminist questions. I include among these: Eugene Borowitz, Choosing a Sex Ethic: A Jewish Inquiry (New York: Schocken, 1969); Lisa Cahill, "Sexual Issues in Christian Theological Ethics: A Review of Recent Studies," Religious Studies Review 4 (January 1978), 1-14; Margaret Farley, "Sexual Ethics," Encyclopedia of Bioethics (New York: Free Press, 1978), 4:1575-89; Anthony Kosnik, et al., Human Sexuality (New York: Paulist, 1977); Peter Laslett, et al., eds., Household and Family in Past Time (Cambridge: Cambridge University Press, 1972); Toward A Quaker View of Sex (London: Friends Service Committee, 1976); Karl Rahner, "Marriage as a Sacrament," Theological Studies, 10 (New York: Herder, 1973), pp. 199-221; Paul Ricoeur, "Wonder Eroticism, and Enigma," Cross Currents 14 (1964), 133-41; Edward Shorter, The Making of the Modern Family (New York: Basic, 1977).

Readings which more explicitly define a feminist perspective can, for purposes of relating them to a course syllabus, be grouped under some general categories. The categories, of course, overlap (since parts of some works address different questions, and since debates, for example, regarding gender and parenting can be incorporated into class sessions either on gender role-differentiation or marriage and family). I will not repeat here works cited previously whose relevance to sexual ethics is obvious (e.g., Harrison); and some works that might well be used in a course in sexual ethics will appear in the bibliographical suggestions I give below for medical ethics.

For *general use* throughout a syllabus, James Nelson's *Embodiment: An Approach to Sexuality and Christian Theology* (Minneapolis, MN: Augsburg, 1978) remains very helpful. There are also some anthologies which include important feminist work on a variety of issues in sexual ethics: R. Baker and F. Elliston, eds., *Philosophy and Sex* (Buffalo, NY: Prometheus, 1975); Alan Soble, ed., *Philosophy of Sex* (Totowa, NJ: Littlefield, Adams, 1980). Discussions of *gender and roles* can profit by readings from: Nancy Chodorow, *The Reproduction of Mothering: Psychoanalysis and the Sociology of Gender* (Berkeley: University of California Press, 1978); Adrienne Rich, *Of Woman Born* (Toronto: Bantam, 1977); Alice Rossi, et al., eds., *The Family* (New York: Norton, 1978); Phyllis Trible, *God and the Rhetoric of Sexuality* (Philadelphia: Fortress, 1978), chaps. 4-6. For class sessions on *same-sex relationships*, helpful essays can be found in Robert Nugent, ed., *A Challenge to Love: Gay and Lesbian Catholics in the Church* (New York: Crossroad, 1983); also, essays in *Christianity and Crisis* (April 4, May 30, and June 13, 1977) offer thoughtful reflections on a variety of questions in this regard. Among the many recent writings in the area of *marriage and family*, the following are of particular note: Jessie Bernard, *The Future of Marriage* (New Haven, CT: Yale University Press, 1972); Walter Brueggemann, "The Covenanted Family: A Zone for Humanness," *Journal of Current Social Issues* 14 (Winter 1977), 18-23; Carl N. Degler, *At Odds: Women and the Family in America from the Revolution to the Present* (Oxford: Oxford University Press, 1980); Barbara Krasner and Margaret Cotroneo, "Essays on Relational Justice," *Foundations* 20 (October-December 1977), 333-51; Kenneth Keniston, *All Our Children* (New York: Harcourt Brace Jovanovich, 1977); Lillian Rubin, *Worlds of Pain* (New York: Basic, 1976); Virginia Tufte and Barbara Myerhoff, eds., *Changing Images of the Family* (New Haven, CT: Yale University Press, 1979). Problems of *abuse of power* in sexual relations can be addressed with the help of: Marie Fortune, *Sexual Violence* (New York: Pilgrim, 1983); Richard Gelles, *Family Violence* (Beverly Hills, CA: Sage, 1979); Susan Brownmiller, *Against Our Will* (New York: Simon and Schuster, 1975); Eva Feder Kittay, "Pornography and the Erotics of Domination," in Gould, pp. 145-74; Judith Berman Brandenburg, "Sexual Harassment in the University: Guidelines for Establishing a Grievance Procedure," *Signs* 8 (Winter 1982), 320-36; Phyllis Crocker, "An Analysis of University Definitions of Sexual Harassment," *Signs* 8 (Summer 1983), 696-707.

Medical Ethics

Feminist studies in medical ethics are still far less numerous than those available for sexual ethics. The one exception is feminist writings on abortion, an issue which, of course, belongs to both areas. The concern of feminists for many problems in medical ethics is growing, however, and it is not difficult to incorporate these concerns into standard medical ethics courses.

The most obvious sets of issues for feminist medical ethics are, perhaps, those which (like abortion) arise out of women's experience of pregnancy and childbirth. These include issues of power and responsibility for reproductive decisions, hence issues of continuing or terminating pregnancy; the development and use of reproductive technology; pre-natal and post-natal medical care; the identification of primary decision-makers and/or processes for adjudicating conflicts between parents, families, infants, medical professionals, and society.

But it is becoming more and more clear that reproductive ethics is not the only area of medicine to generate feminist questions. Whether we look at structural issues regarding the delivery of medical care, or frontier ethical issues regarding specific forms of medical treatment, the methods and principles of feminist ethics are immediately relevant. The general elements of feminist ethics that I have noted above have direct bearing on current issues in medical ethics. Thus, for example, the commitment to combined principles of autonomy and mutuality offers an obvious vantage point for participation in growing debates about the centrality, yet limits, of the requirement of informed consent. A feminist preference for collaborative models of working relationships makes inevitable a feminist critique of rigid hierarchicalization among health care providers. Feminist concerns for new interpretations of human "embodiment" yield revisionist proposals for whole-person health care. Feminist opposition to sexism, classism, and racism renders necessary a critical analysis of the problems of society writ large in the world of the hospital and in the general system of health care delivery in this country.

The growing attention that feminists are giving to issues of medical ethics comes, then, from fairly obvious coincidences of speculative and practical interests and concerns; but it comes, also, from the simple fact that women constitute a majority of health care providers as well as recipients. Feminists cannot sustain a focus on women's experience without taking larger and larger account of the experience of the need for and provision of medical care. Specific issues which have thus far drawn the attention of feminists include the medical care of the elderly; medical settings for childbirth; issues of pregnancy termination; the use of amniocentesis for gender selection; conflict between traditional roles and newly perceived responsibilities of nurses; models of physician-patient relationship in a culture and in relation to a profession marked by sexism; psychiatric treatment for women; etc.

The first way, therefore, in which feminist ethical approaches can be incorporated into courses in medical ethics is by raising the kinds of questions that feminist ethics as such tends to raise. The general literature we have already seen in that regard is here relevant. The following bibliographical resources, however, provide examples of some specific applications already made.

The May 1982, issue of *The Journal of Medicine and Philosophy*, under the editorship of Caroline Whitbeck, focused on "Women and Medicine." It provides an overview of issues and some essays on specific topics such as health delivery systems, psychiatric discourse, and problems in childbirth. Other general sources for feminist medical ethics include: Margaret Farley, "Feminist Theology and Issues in Bioethics," forthcoming in E. Shelp, ed., *Theology and Medicine* (D. Reidel); Claudia Dreifus, ed., *Seizing Our Bodies: The Politics of Women's Health* (New York: Random House, 1977); B. K. Rothman, "Women, Health, and Medicine" in J. Freeman, ed., *Women: A Feminist Perspective* (Palo Alto, CA: Mayfield, 1979), pp. 27-40.

As an example of literature available on a specific topic, the following writings focus on the issue of the development and use of reproductive technology: Shulamith Firestone, in *The Dialectic of Sex* (New York: Bantam, 1971), and Juliet Mitchell, in *Women's Estate* (New York: Vintage, 1971), provide two sides to the question of the value of technology for freeing women from the negative aspects of the experience of reproduction. Problems in the medicalization of childbirth are analyzed in: M. Daly, *Gyn/Ecology*; A. Oakley, "A Case of Maternity," *Signs* 4 (1979), 606-31; A. Rich, *Of Woman Born*; R. W. Wertz and D. C. Wertz, *Lying-In: A History of Childbirth in America* (New York: Free Press, 1977). Varying analyses of maternal consciousness, of reproductive responsibility on the part of women and men, and of the use and misuse of technology in this area emerge in: J. B. Elshtain, "A Feminist Agenda on Reproductive Technology," *Hastings Center Report* 12 (1982), 40-43; Farley, "Feminist Theology and Issues in Bioethics"; Harrison, *Our Right to Choose*; Karen Lebacqz, "Reproductive Research and the Image of Woman" in C. B. Fischer, *et al.*, eds., *Women in a Strange Land* (Philadelphia: Fortress, 1975); Mary O'Brien, *The Politics of Reproduction* (London: Routledge & Kegan Paul, 1981).

The Journal of Philosophy and Medicine volume cited above provides some basis for selecting course readings and formulating bibliographies on other specific issues, such as ethics and nursing, feminist issues for psychiatric ethics, etc.

One should not, I think, end an essay on the incorporation of feminist questions into an ethics curriculum without some word about feminist pedagogical concerns. That is, whatever bibliography is used, and whatever issues are addressed, feminist ethics points to a preferred context for teaching and learning where participants are co-learners; where experience can be drawn from across racial, religious, and national boundaries; and where interdisciplinary resources are sought and welcomed for the understanding of this experience.

8

THE FEMINIST TURN IN SOCIAL ETHICS

Daniel C. Maguire

Anyone who plies the noble art-science of social ethics (moral theology, Christian ethics), while taking no account of the feminist turn of consciousness, is open to charges of professional irresponsibility and incompetence. No. That is not an overstatement or an overblown rhetorical lead-in. The history of ethics is turning an epochal corner. To miss the turn is to be lost and useless.[1]

Feminism is concerned with the shift in roles and the question of the rights that have been unjustly denied women. But all of that, however important and even essential, is secondary. The main event is epistemological. Changes in *what* we know are normal; changes in *how* we know are revolutionary. Feminism is a challenge to the way we have gone about *knowing*. The epistemological *terra firma* of the recent past is rocking and as the event develops, it promises to change the face of the earth.

The main impact of feminism will be felt in the area of moral knowledge. That, of course, is broader than ethics since all of the social sciences are heavy with moral assumptions and evaluations. Economics, politics (simplistically called political science), education, journalism, business administration, engineering, *et al.* are all intra-familial siblings of social ethics, although educational systems have treated them as separable strangers. (This mischievous separation, indeed, is a natural target of the emerging feminist consciousness.)

Feminism, however, addresses itself most directly to social ethics. Every category and tool of this discipline is touched by this new awareness. Before I argue and try to show that this is the case, an obstacle is present and should be faced.

Conversion and In-Depth Knowing

The new feminine consciousness reaches the affective depths of moral knowledge. *Learning* about it is not like learning about a new

[1] Aside from Marjorie, my wife, who is cited in the text, my advisory committee for this article included Judith and Bill Kelsey who while specializing in Christology on their way to Marquette doctorates are majoring in feminism together; and Fran Leap whose dissertation on the contributions of feminism to Christian ethics, will, with the help of God and the permission of new baby Aloysius, be completed within a year at Marquette.

Daniel C. Maguire, Professor in the Department of Theology, Marquette University (Milwaukee, WI 53233), has written extensively in many areas of ethics. His most recent book from Crossroad is The New Subversives. He is immediate past President of the Society of Christian Ethics.

medical procedure or a new approach to mathematics. It involves conversion and a shift of horizons that can bring considerable pain and threat. Here is where insight involves investment, and where knowing and vocation unite. To call someone to feminist reappraisal we would be well advised to mimic the fair warnings of the gospels in announcing their new and good news. *Metanoiete* is the first cry of Mark's Gospel. It is often translated "repent," but that misses the challenge. It is a call for a new *nous*, a radically new mind and outlook that is not simply achieved. To achieve it it would be necessary to raise up all the valleys of the mind and to level all our mountainous presuppositions. The axe must go to the roots of our old views, so that a new heaven and a new earth will present themselves to our consciences. Indeed, the shift is such that it can be compared to reentering one's mother's womb and being born again. With some persons, it indeed might seem hopeless. One can be tempted to say that we might as well leave the dead to bury the dead. The impossible is impossible. You can't get a camel through the eye of a needle. But, yet, with God, all things are possible. And so the feminist challenge must be issued.

I once heard Gabriel Marcel, the French existentialist philosopher, speaking at the University of Pennsylvania. In his youth, Marcel had had great antipathy toward religion. Later religion was to become a major concern in his work. Someone asked him how such a dramatic shift had come to be. His answer was dogmatically existentialist: "Through personal encounters. Nothing else ever changes anyone in any important way." The change from sexist-patriarchical to feminist and eventually inclusively humanistic thinking is massive. No simple argument will achieve it. An old saying from Latin Christianity comes relevantly to mind: "It is not through logic that God's salvation reaches us." (*Non in dialectica complacuit Deo salvum facere populum suum.*) Personal, grace-filled encounters must play their crucial role. We must be open to the *kairos*, the moment of opportunity.

Geoffrey Wood once compared a *kairos* to a log jam. All kinds of logs coming from all kinds of places suddenly come together. When they are together like this they will support your weight. No single one of them would do so. The *kairos* is the moment when many influences coalesce into a saving unity and a new bouyancy. To switch metaphors, it affords a new horizon by reason of which nothing ever looks the same again. In simple language, something clicks, and we are "a new creature."

The conversion may be dramatic or it may be subtle like the slow light-growth of early dawn. In the latter case, we may not be quite able to say at which moment it became day. The conversion experience is needed not just by men since women too have drunk the social poisons of sexism and come to believe in their own inferiority. Elsewise they could not be so tolerant of their banishment from the mainstreams of power and life.

It will not be amiss for me to recount here the conversion experience of one woman which came about with dramatic suddenness. The woman is my conjugal colleague and the story (given with permission) is this: some years ago, Margie was not a feminist. When asked if she were a feminist, she would reply: "No. Dan is!" Then two popes died in quick succession and the stage for conversion was interestingly set. Our television was filled with *papalia*. Two elaborate funerals and two prolonged installations. Our two-year old son, Tommy, resented our absorption in the papal events since even Sesame Street was proscribed during those hours. But he joined us and caught the spirit of the moment. At one point, he left us, went to the kitchen, got his red Cheerios bowl, plopped it upon his little head and announced: "I a pope!"

How lovely it is when grace comes in merry moments. Margie was struck by Tommy's endearingly immodest ambition. It was so normal and so refreshing. Childhood requires no limits to the imagination. The whole world must be the child's imaginative oyster. He/she must think they can be anything. As the richness of reality unfolds to them they must feel that they can have a go at all of it. The limits will eventually be felt, but in that early budding of consciousness, all doors must be seen as open to the hopeful imaging of the child. At that point Tommy had a moral right to hear that indeed he might be pope, or Easter Bunny, or snow plow driver or any of his already announced ambitions. But, it struck Margie with lightning strength and suddenness, that if Tommy were a girl he would have to hear sooner or later that he could not be pope or many other things—merely because of being a girl. The world would not be as open to him. Then Margie looked to the television set and saw the scene there in a new light. Only men were at the throne of God. Masculinity was the sacrament of encounter with a God who was also conceived as male. Actual barriers had been constructed for the occasion to separate women from the holy place. It struck her that there was a message on that screen about her mother and her three sisters and about the daughter she hoped she would one day have and about herself. A feminist was born!

The story illustrates many things (not the least of which is that popes do not die in vain). No new information was available to Margie at that moment. She had heard it all. She had read feminist literature. But she had been inured, and now she was receptive. "Whereas I was blind now I see" (Jn 9:25). The mystical core of her being, where moral knowledge is born in an affective appreciation of personal and terrestrial life, had been reached. Indentured rationalizations had been pierced and she was now free to hurt for herself and for her sisters and to rise from that hurt to new life. And it all began with a Cheerios bowl on a delightful little head.

Conversion is a process that does not end. He/she who claims to be a feminist and without sin in the area of sexism is a liar. (The same is true of racism and class elitism.) To dare to teach ethics is to accept a professional commitment to ongoing conversion. We can't just "bone up" on feminist thought; we have to "heart in" on it. "I believe, Lord: help my unbelief," is the posture of an honest searcher in the field of ethics.[2] Teilhard was right when he said that all research is worship. Ethical research is manifestly such. Macho-masculine scholarship needs to learn that. It was too smug and cocksure of itself, too abstracted and too tut-tuttingly tolerant of the male-made problems we study in the world and in the Church. Feminism is *the* major event in ethical theory of our day. Macho-masculine scholarship must come here, not as to a well intentioned and laudable side-show, but as to the most brightly burning bush on the theological and ethical horizon today. No ethics will be profound or holy that does not come, sandals removed, to this blessed place.

The Epistemological Revolution

The subtlest form of sexism is to see feminism as a woman's issue. It is a human issue of first order importance for social ethics. Feminism represents a reappraisal of (1) the nature of nature; (2) the nature of person; (3) the linkage of private and public morality; (4) the plight of technologized rationality which has humanity at the brink of disaster; and (5) the sources of theological ethics.

(1) *Nature*. Feminism calls us from a two-nature to a one-nature ethics. As Beverly Harrison writes: "Thomas Aquinas argued, following Aristotle, that male female 'nature' differed because biological structure differed. This two-nature idea runs deep in Christian theology."[3] The heresy here is one of division. Male and female were we made; in God's image, that is, were we made. Macho-masculine scholarship split the human molecule, degrading the feminine component and perverting the masculine into a dominator. Permit me to quote something I wrote elsewhere: "If the essential human molecule is dyadic, male/female, the perversion of one part of the dyad perverts the other. And, to distort femininity *and* masculinity, the constitutive ingredients of humanity, is to distort humanity itself; nothing will be spared the fallout from so radical a corruption. Here is *original* sin. Here is the fundamental lie that will have to mark all human ideas, customs, and institutions."[4] From disarmament to abortion, there is no moral problem that presents itself to

[2] On the role of belief in moral knowledge see my *The Moral Choice* (Minneapolis, MN: Winston, 1979), chapter 3.

[3] Beverly Wildung Harrison, "The Power of Anger in the Work of Love: Christian Ethics for Women and Other Strangers," *Union Seminary Quarterly Review 36* (Supplementary 1981), 57. See also, Rosemary Ruether's newest contribution, *Sexism and God-Talk: Toward a Feminist Theology* (Boston: Beacon, 1983).

[4] Daniel C. Maguire, "The Feminization of God and Ethics," *Christianity and Crisis 43* (March 15, 1982), 59.

"the valuing animal," as Nietzsche called us, that does not bear the mark of this sexist perversion of nature.[5]

(2) *Person.* Person as such does not exist. Only boys and girls, men and women exist. Person, unsexed, is a figment of the imagination. Yet person is a key term of modern moral discourse. A two-nature ethics, however, could not bring clarity to the term. Such an ethics could only offer an isolationist concept of person, lacking in the relational and sharing aspects of a more realistic personology. Harsh individualism results. God becomes "wholly other," and human persons become autonomous and self-possessed by definition. Again Beverly Harrison with a feminist correction: "The ecologists have recently reminded us of what nurturers always knew—that we are part of a *web of life* so intricate as to be beyond our comprehension."[6] (See Margaret Farley's radically suggestive essay: "New Patterns of Relationship: Beginnings of a Moral Revolution." Sister Margaret is a member of the Sisters of Mercy, an order of women that has suffered much of late from macho-Vatican oppression. Think of that as you read her and pray for "clicks" of conversion in high places. See also, by that convert to feminism, Marjorie Reiley Maguire, "Personhood, Covenant, and Abortion," for a bold and original new view of personhood. The discussion is illustrated by reference to the abortion question, but its meaning goes beyond.[7])

(3) *Linkage of Private and Public Morality.* When we split the human molecule and relegated women to truncated personhood, we also ghettoed the qualities associated with woman. (A pedestal is a clean ghetto.) Trust, affectivity, caring, nurturing, identification with children and their needs were deemed party to the frailty of woman. Then we handed politics over to those whose socialization disparaged those "womanly" qualities. The result is a planet in terminal peril, with "third" and "fourth" worlds full of hunger, and more than a million dollars every thirty seconds spent on military fantasies and plans. By the fruits of macho-masculine politics we shall know macho-masculine men. Men are the warriors of the species—the Amazons are but a myth—and war is not the extension of statecraft, but its collapse. There have been 150 wars since World War II and 4,000,000 men are involved in battle throughout the world at this writing, according to The Center for Defense Information. Macho-masculine politics stands embarrassed.

[5]Perhaps the most helpful book showing the pervasive poison of sexism infecting issues such as racism, anti-Semitism, classism, religion, even psychoanalysis and ecology is Rosemary Radford Ruether's *New Woman New Earth* (New York: Seabury, 1975).

[6]Harrison, p. 50.

[7]Margaret A. Farley, R.S.M., "New Patterns of Relationship: Beginnings of a Moral Revolution," *Theological Studies* 36 (December 1975), 627-46, and Marjorie Reiley Maguire, "Personhood, Covenant, and Abortion," in *The Annual of the Society of Christian Ethics, 1983*, ed. Joseph Allen (Waterloo, Ontario: The Council on the Study of Religion, 1983).

So, too, macho-economics. Unfortunately, a dehumanized masculinity has been the seedbed of our controlling metaphors and symbols in economics, in political theory, and in social ethics. The fact that politics and economics are servants for the *nurturing* of life—that they are by nature *caring* enterprises, has been missed. (The arms race and Reaganomics are the natural issue of such deviance.)

When a healed masculine and feminine blend into a fruitfully inclusive humanism, all the disciplines and professions that deal with the polity will be unified around a theory of justice. Macho-masculine social science has excommunicated as femininely tainted many of the qualities of a *just* society. Ironically, a truly and excitingly humanistic theory of justice has lain all too fallow in the pages of the Jewish and Christian scriptures. (Toward a recovery of biblical justice, read Stephen Charles Mott's *Biblical Ethics and Social Change*, particularly chapters four and five, and my "The Primacy of Justice in Moral Theology."[8]

(4) *Technologized Rationality.* One terrible story symbolizes the problem here. It is planned that in the Christmas season of 1983, we will station our Cruise and Pershing II missiles in Europe. The Cruise, if it works as designed, will skip ingeniously over mountains, hovering close to the earth below the scanning eyes of radar. The Pershing II can strike its Russian targets some six minutes after launch. With their installation, the "hot line" becomes irrelevant. Launch on Warning, or automated reaction, becomes the new command system of Soviet warcraft. Moral choice is abdicated to the machine—in this case, the Soviet electronic machine, which is less sophisticated (as men say) than ours. Rationality yields to a second rate technology. Specifically human wisdom, which by its nature cannot be machinized or computerized, is undone. Politics moves to second place and the world teeters on the brink of computer error that can end the world.

Let me underline the inherent madness of this parable of technologized rationality. We hide our computer secrets from the Soviets for reasons of alleged security. But if we install these unstoppable missiles, we will have to start a massive lend lease program to give all our technical knowledge to the Soviets so their inferior equipment will not mistakenly signal an attack and launch the salvoes that end the world.

In symbol form we have here the eschaton of technologized rationality. If human intelligence is patterned on machination, then machination in some form may replace human intelligence. So it has happened. (The computer is, after all, *Time*'s Man of the Year.) We are empowered

[8] Stephen Charles Mott, *Biblical Ethics and Social Change* (New York: Oxford, 1982), and Daniel C. Maguire, "The Primacy of Justice in Moral Theology," *Horizons* 10 (Spring, 1983), 72-85. Also, I do not hesitate to recommend my *A New American Justice* (Minneapolis, MN: Winston, 1982), esp. pp. 53-124.

by our personhood to choose life or to choose death. That power is passing to the mechanical Man of the Year. The reductionistic technologizing of rationality is complete.

Feminism is curative for this kind of mind-default. It brings on a holistic epistemology. It eschews "the intellectualistic fallacy"[9] and takes account of affectivity as the animating mold of moral knowing. It leads to embodied rationality which shies from the sacrifice of flesh to abstraction.

(5) *The Theological Sources*. Human knowing is an event in which the knower both receives and gives. To know is to interpret, a word that comes from the Latin *interpres*. An *interpres* is a broker, a negotiator, an agent who arranges a bargain between two parties. The *interpres* in Christian exegesis and historical studies has been a male, and usually a subtly or bluntly sexist male. The bargains struck by such brokers are up for reevaluation. Clearly, not all exegesis done by men is suspect, but the healing supplement to male labors in this field is now arriving. Insightful scholars like Elisabeth Shüssler Fiorenza, Phyllis Trible, Sandra Schneiders, Elaine Pagels, to mention only a few, are bringing new grace and perspective to the study of the *sacra pagina*. Read them with good appetite.

Conclusion

Every man and woman doing feminist studies is contributing to social ethics. Our discipline is affected every time they lift a pen or offer a challenge, whether they are working in scripture, history, systematic theology, or beyond. Feminist retooling by all social ethicists is simply mandatory. If there is a burden here, it is sweet and rewarding. Let what Madonna Kolbenschlag says in her *Kiss Sleeping Beauty Good-Bye* be our last word: "The faith that is expressed here, and that is asked of women and men who would be truly free, is not backward-looking or nostalgic; nor is it blindly iconoclastic and memoryless. It nurtures the seed of our future becoming in the revelation of the present, in a tradition that remains faithful to itself by transcending itself."[10]

[9] See my "Ratio practica and Intellectualistic Fallacy," *The Journal of Religious Ethics* 10 (Spring, 1982), 22-39.
[10] Madonna Kolbenschlag, *Kiss Sleeping Beauty Good-Bye: Breaking the Spell of Feminine Myths and Models* (Garden City, NY: Doubleday, 1979), p. xiv.